BLOODY B

HISTO

BRIGHTON

C000126952

BLOODY BRITISH HISTORY
HISTORY

BRIGHTON

DAVID J. BOYNE

The
History
Press

*With special thanks to Chris Stone, Mark Howell, Carl Salton-Cox,
Russel Rose, Hannah Rose Tranter, Tess McNally-Watson, Tanay Sharma,
Beverley Green, Juanita Hall and Cate Ludlow for their kind assistance ...
... and a fond farewell to the Brighton History Centre.*

First published in 2013

The History Press
The Mill, Brimscombe Port
Stroud, Gloucestershire, GL5 2QG
www.thehistorypress.co.uk

© David J. Boyne, 2013

The right of David J. Boyne to be identified as the Author
of this work has been asserted in accordance with the
Copyright, Designs and Patents Act 1988.

British Library Cataloguing in Publication Data.
A catalogue record for this book is available from the British Library.

ISBN 978 0 7524 9082 3

Typesetting and origination by The History Press
Printed in Great Britain

CONTENTS

100,000,000 BC–AD 410

FROM PRIMORDIAL ALGAE TO THE ROMANS

BRIGHTON IS A shortened version of the older Saxon place name Brighthelmstone. Thus in one sense Brighton has only been around since the Saxons arrived just over 1,500 years ago. There have, however, been many previous occupants in and around Brighton and Sussex that are equally a part of its history, so by way of introduction this opening section will briefly consider the first 100 million years of life here, from primordial algae to the Romans.

The most permanent impact on Brighton and its landscape has been that left by its very first inhabitants, the microscopic green plankton that lived here 100 million years ago. Back then it wasn't just the place where the Downs met the sea – it was the sea. The Downs are actually the remains of those first residents, compressed in their centillions on the seabed over millions of years, to form the chalk that we see today.

The Romans may have left the odd road, the walls of Pevensey Fort, and the marvellous mosaics at Fishbourne Palace as evidence of their occupation,

but the scale of their legacy pales into insignificance in comparison to the majestic landscape bequeathed to us by these little green creatures. Indeed, given the use of chalk in the construction industry in recent centuries, it is even possible to suggest that the plankton have also had a far greater impact on the built environment than the Romans. Around 65 million years ago, as the dinosaurs became extinct, the plankton moved away to new waters.

Humanoids arrived considerably later, although then, as now, Sussex appears to have been a popular location. Taking advantage of the improving climate between glaciations, an ancestor of ours known as *Homo heidlebergensis* had

The chalk cliffs at Ovingdean. (Tanay Sharma)

moved into West Sussex some 500,000 years ago. Boxgrove man, as he has become known, lived on the beach and appears to have enjoyed an early version of the Atkins diet, rich in animal protein.

Several ice ages and 300,000 years later our more recent cousins, the Neanderthals, were camping on a beach in Brighton behind the Marina. Without the benefit of the present-day Asda store they also lived a hunter-gatherer lifestyle, as is testified by the wealth of butchered animal remains that have been found in the same layers from 200,000 years ago. On the menu for *Homo sapiens neanderthalensis* were a range of delicacies, including mammoth, woolly rhinoceros, bison and whale. Whilst the hunting of the big land mammals must have taken some considerable expertise and coordination, it has to be assumed that the whale was a more opportunistic find that had been washed up on the beach.

The final influx of nomadic hunter-gatherers followed the retreating ice of the most recent glacial event, and arrived in Sussex from 8,000 BC, during the Mesolithic era, having walked across

Mammoth on the menu for Neanderthal man. (Titus 332)

what is now the English Channel. There are about half a dozen major clusters of flint tools and objects found from this period in the county, one of which is around Brighton.

At about 4,300 BC the Neolithic period began, typified by a new more settled approach to Stone Age living. With the domestication of animals and the growing of crops these people could now live more permanently in the same location, leaving surplus time and energy to start constructing more comfortable dwellings and ever more ambitious monuments.

Whitehawk Camp is one of the earliest, largest and most complex examples of such a communal monument to be found in northern Europe, and dates back to around 3,500 BC. Set on a hilltop, with commanding views as far as the Isle of Wight, it consists of a series of circular ditches and banks with several entrances. Unfortunately much of it is now variously obscured by allotments, the pulling up section of Brighton racecourse, and perhaps most thoughtlessly by part of a late twentieth-century housing estate. The discovery of a hearth containing the fragments of skulls belonging to five young people, aged between 5 and 20, suggests there may have been human sacrifices, or even cannibalism, on the site.

With the arrival of the Bronze Age in the 3rd millennium BC, settlements sprouted up all over the area, particularly on the Downs. Evidence of such dwellings has been found at Mile Oak,

PILTDOWN MAN

Forgery is a common part of living in the present day. From dodgy £20 notes and equine beef-burgers to fake designer jeans, we are surrounded by fraudulent misrepresentation. None of these examples, however, can match the longevity and influence of the greatest fake in the history of Sussex – the Piltdown Man.

On his discovery by Charles Dawson in 1912, he was claimed to be the missing link between apes and men, dating back several million years. Dawson had taken a few skull fragments to the Geological Society, and as a result was accompanied by a British Museum scientist to the Piltdown Pit for further excavations. On this survey more parts, including a jawbone, were found, but it seemed only Dawson had his eye in and he made all of the finds.

There was a mixed response from the scientific world, with British scholars generally being more accepting than those from America or Europe. The British scientists had wanted Piltdown Man to be real, so it was much easier to fool them. As a result of the importance given to the 'discovery', other genuine finds were ignored for nearly half a century. The hoax went on until 1953, when the skull was identified as being from a medieval-period human, the jaw from an orang-utan that had lived 500 years previously in Sumatra, with the teeth belonging to a fossilised chimp. The bones had been dyed and the teeth filed.

This was not the first time that Dawson had been creative with the construction of ancient history. He had in his collection a range of fake articles far more numerous than any pre-Christmas stall on Western Road could muster. Chinese vases, Roman statues, and the Brighton 'Toad in the Hole', a toad that had apparently been encased in a flint nodule, were all part of his repertoire. They were all about as real as a £20 Rolex.

Having examined Dawson's life and collections, author and archaeologist Miles Russell told the BBC that 'Piltdown was not a one-off hoax, more the culmination of a life's work'.

West Blatchington, Patcham, Plumpton Plain, Coldean Lane and Varley Halls.

What have become known as Iron Age hill forts dominate the Downs around Brighton and were originally thought to be purely defensive in nature. Devil's Dyke, Thunderbarrow Hill, Ditchling Beacon and Hollingbury Hill provide examples of such structures. In recent years both their age and their purpose have come increasingly into question. Many of these features were already in use during the later Bronze Age period and it has been suggested that they may also have served as administrative and residential centres for the Iron Age aristocracy.

The progress from stone to bronze and then iron-based cultures was probably the result of the same long-standing inhabitants adapting to novel technologies, in much the same way that we have adopted mobile phones and computers. In the first century BC a new wave of Celtic peoples, the Belgae, started arriving on the shores of England, driven along in front of the expanding Roman Empire.

Hollingbury Iron Age Hill Fort – the golf course came later. (Reproduced with the kind permission of the Royal Pavilion and Museums: Brighton and Hove)

The Atrebates took up residence in Sussex, and their kingdom stretched beyond the current county borders into both Kent and Hampshire. Their domain was far larger than that of the British chieftains who had ruled from the hilltops, and the centre of administration moved to an urban settlement known as an oppidum, which for the Atrebates was probably on the coastal plain near Chichester. They also introduced coins as means of exchange, although it is unclear as to whether this welcome innovation was accompanied by an embryonic banking industry.

Julius Caesar avoided Sussex when he raided Britain in 55 and 54 BC, although it is believed that he was on good terms with Commius, the King of the Atrebates, at that time. They would later fall out when Commius supported the rebellion of Vercingetorix in Gaul, and he was fortunate in evading the Roman Army and escaping back to Sussex. This was a temporary upset however, and in the years before the full Roman invasion of Britain in AD 43, a number of his descendants would seek and receive the sanctuary of the Emperor in Rome, at times of internecine strife back home.

The Romans brought a long period of stability to the region, leaving a rich inheritance in West Sussex where the city of Chichester was the largest settlement, connected to London by Stane Street. To the east lay a more agricultural hinterland, although villas from the period have been found near Preston Park in Brighton and at Southwick, whilst Stanmer Park was home to a Roman temple.

The Pax Romana started to break down after AD 270, and the villa at Preston Park was burned down around this time. The great 'Barbarian conspiracy' of AD 367, when the province was invaded by Picts, Scots, Attacotti, Franks and Saxons, aided and abetted by an assortment of slaves, deserters and discontents from within, was the writing on the wall for Roman Britain. Although order was eventually restored, within a few years the Empire contracted back to the Continent, and the time of the Saxons began.

THE KINGDOM OF THE SOUTH SAXONS

Slaughter, Sanctity and Slavery

DURING THE THIRD and fourth centuries pirates from the north of Europe had started raiding the British coastline, leading to the strengthening of defences along what was called the Saxon Shore, which stretched from the Wash to the west country. Even before the official Roman withdrawal from Britain in AD 410, Germanic troops were being used both in the Roman Legions and as mercenaries in the defence of the province.

By the middle of the fifth century these mercenaries, perhaps dissatisfied with the going rate for their services, and encouraged both by the weakness of the Britons and the wealth of their lands, had started to invite over their friends and families. In around AD 455, Hengist and Horsta, former mercenaries employed by Vortigern, the leader of the Britons, arrived from Jutland to establish a kingdom in Kent.

In 477 the Saxons wanted a piece of the action, and Aelle landed with three ships on the coast of Sussex, somewhere near Selsey Bill. Here, according to the *Anglo-Saxon Chronicle*, 'they slew

many of the Welsh', before driving the survivors, in an early version of ethnic cleansing, into the then wild and densely forested Weald.

As Aelle moved slowly eastwards across the modern county, in 485 he ran into a counter-attack from the obstinate Britons (or Welsh, as the *Chronicle* also referred to them, reflecting the geographical location that they had been driven into by the Anglo-Saxons at the time of writing) on the banks of a river known as Mearcredsburn. Whilst there is still some doubt as to the actual location of this battle, local folklore has it taking place on Slonk Hill to the north-east of Shoreham.

This was but a temporary setback for Aelle and his men, and by 491 they were besieging the last outpost of the Britons in coastal Sussex, at the old Roman fort of Pevensey. In due course the isolated defenders were overrun, and according to the *Chronicle*, Aelle proceeded to 'slew all that were therein; nor was one Briten left there afterwards'.

For the next two centuries the South Saxons carried on quite happily in their pagan ways, their isolation largely allowing them to avoid the internecine wars between the larger, and now largely Christian, kingdoms of Wessex, East Anglia, Mercia and Northumbria. Their near neighbours in Kent had been the first to accept this second Roman incursion, although the still dense forests of the Weald provided an impenetrable barrier to the spread of Catholicism into the still pagan Sussex. Both peace and paganism were to be rudely displaced in the latter part of the seventh century, with St Wilfrid of Ripon playing a leading role.

Appropriately enough he had first come across the pagan South Saxons in the year 666. He was returning from a visit to the Continent when his ship was blown off course and beached on the coast of Sussex. The locals were less than welcoming and attacked the stranded party, leading to a battle in which Wilfred and his retinue had to fight for their lives. During this struggle the South Saxon host was repelled with many dead, including their high priest, whilst Wilfred successfully escaped on the incoming tide.

Harold II is crowned, the last King of the Saxons. (Myrabella)

By the time he returned in 680, the Sussex shore was a little more welcoming. The new King Aethelwalh had married a Christian wife, and had himself converted a few years previously. Furthermore, Wilfrid's arrival coincided with the end of a severe drought that the pagan gods had been unable to resolve. So dreadful were the conditions that, according to Bede, groups of up to fifty starving people would jump from the cliffs to their deaths, to escape their desperate circumstances.

Such dire conditions left the inhabitants in a much more receptive frame of mind to this new god who brought the rains with him. Wilfrid also introduced new methods of fishing that not only alleviated the famine and aided in the conversion, but also pioneered the development of the industry upon which the settlement at Brighthelmstone would come to be based for the next 1,000 years.

The return to a time of plenty soon attracted the attentions of a West Saxon noble, Caedwalla, who was in exile in the Weald. His forces ravaged Sussex, killing King Aethelwalh, before being repulsed. Whilst in Sussex he had met Wilfrid, and was so impressed that he too converted to the new religion. Having become King of Wessex, Caedwalla returned with a vengeance, and put the South Saxons into a state of slavery.

In 686 he also attacked the last remaining heathen outpost, on the Isle of Wight, slaughtering or enslaving the whole population from King Aruald downwards. In keeping with Caedwalla's new faith, Aruald's two sons were duly baptised, before being duly executed. As part of the resettlement of the island, Wilfrid was awarded 300 hides of land and a share of the booty, although to his credit he did release several hundred slaves who had been awarded to him.

SLAVERY

Slavery was endemic during this period, frequently the by-product of an economy in which warfare and raiding played a large part. One such victim was a young girl of pagan background, and thus probably from Sussex, named Balthildis. In 641 she was sold for a low price to an official at the Merovingian court in Francia, where she converted to Christianity and attracted the attentions of Clovis II. She married him and became Queen of the Frankish kingdom of Neustria, and later assisted her sons Clothar and Childeric in their accession to the thrones of Neustria and Austrasia.

Harold II dies at the Battle of Hastings. (Myrabella)

Despite her elevated status she never forgot her origins, and was an early campaigner against slavery, using her power to pass laws against enslavement and the associated export trade. As well as being renowned for her generosity to the poor, she also used her new wealth to buy many of her kin out of bondage. Despite such efforts slavery would continue to be a large factor in the medieval economy, and contributed in no small part to the wealth of a later Saxon family of Sussex origins, the Godwines.

THERE'S A SAXON IN MY KITCHEN

There was a shock in store for the builders renovating the kitchen of a house on Exeter Street a few years ago. As they were preparing to lay a new floor and digging down to the foundations, they uncovered a skeleton. Concerned that this might be a *Brookside*-style scenario, the police were called in. However, a team from the coroner's office rapidly concluded that it was not a recent burial.

Archaeologists examined the bones and concluded that they belonged to a Saxon woman from around AD 800, and that it was just one of many similar burials found in that area. The remains were removed to a local museum and the builders were soon renovating the kitchen on a brand new floor.

AD 1000–1086

THE NORMAN CONQUEST

(1066 and Before That)

THE YEAR 1066 is probably the best known and yet the least understood in English history, with William the Conqueror's close-fought victory at the Battle of Hastings commonly seen as marking the end of the Anglo-Saxon era and its replacement with Norman rule. Such neat dividing lines rarely bear close scrutiny, and this particular generalisation is no exception, as a brief examination of the monarchy in the preceding sixty-six years of the eleventh century will illustrate.

William's coronation on Christmas Day, 1066 made him the tenth King of England since the millennium. Until Edward the Confessor's death earlier that year, there had been eight kings, four of whom were Anglo-Saxon and four who were the leaders of the Vikings, who had resumed their bloody raids in the latter part of the tenth century.

As the crown switched backwards and forwards from Anglo-Saxon to Viking to Anglo-Saxon several times, some continuity was provided by Emma of Normandy. She was the daughter of Richard the Fearless, Duke of Normandy.

Emma was the wife of two kings (Aethelred the Unready and Cnut), step-mother to two more (Edmund Ironside and Harold Harefoot), and also the birth mother of King Harthacnut and Edward the Confessor.

Perhaps unsurprisingly in this complex familial line, she was also given the English name of Aelfgifu, which was the same as that of the two different mothers of her royal stepsons. They were the first wives of Aethelred and Cnut, although helpfully one was from York and the other from Northampton. To go full circle in this complex web of Viking and Anglo Saxon dynastic relations, Emma/Aelfgifu was also the great aunt of William the Conqueror.

Despite the marriage of his sister Edith to Edward the Confessor, the only king who didn't have a direct place within this convoluted family tree was Harold Godwineson, although he was reputed to have been betrothed to William's daughter Adeliza whilst in Normandy. Harold's Danish mother Gytha Thorksidda had also been the sister-in-law of Cnut.

Pevensey Castle, built by the Normans inside the Roman fort. (Piotr Zarobkiewicz at en.wikimedia)

Whilst the above genealogical discussion might seem to indicate a family feud more than an epochal change, the actions of the last king of the Wessex royal line, the half Norman Edward the Confessor, suggest that Norman incursions into the ruling class of England had begun well before 1066. Both at court and in the Church, Edward had sought to balance the power of his English nobles, led by the Earl Godwine, by appointing Normans where possible.

Furthermore, concerned by the unruly Welsh, he had imported French relatives and granted them lands on the border, where they proceeded to build stone castles in the Norman style. In an early conflict with the Godwine dynasty one of these Frenchmen, Ralph of Mantes, was awarded the lands of his local rival, Harold's older brother

Sweyn. Sweyn had been exiled after he had kidnapped and raped the Abbess of Leominster. The relationship between Edward and the Godwines was rarely harmonious, and at various times they almost went to war. Given these fractious relations, it would have been surprising had Edward not promised the kingdom to William upon his death.

When Edward eventually died without an heir in January 1066, Harold rubber-stamped the old maxim that possession is nine-tenths of the law, by getting the agreement of the assembled nobles to his coronation. This went down like a lead balloon with his rival claimants, William of Normandy and, representing the Scandinavian side of the family, Harald Hardrada of Norway.

Harold had spent the summer on the south coast awaiting the expected attack

THE ARCHITECTURE OF NORMAN POWER

Sussex was crucial to the new rulers, being just across the Channel from their home base in Normandy. The old Saxon burghs of Sussex became Norman Rapes, each with its own stone castle to demonstrate the power and authority of the new regime.

In the post-Conquest period these imposing structures were built to protect the coast and cover river crossings at Hastings, Pevensey, Lewes, Bramber and Arundel, endowing the county with a rich, if at the time unpopular, Norman heritage.

Arundel Castle. (Farwestern)

from Normandy. Having released many of his troops to take in the harvest, he was caught off balance as Hardrada struck first, attacking in the north with the assistance of Harold's exiled brother, Tostig Godwineson. Recruiting as he went, Harold marched to York in about ten days, and on 25 September destroyed the Norwegians in a surprise attack, killing Harald and Tostig in the process.

As Harold marched wearily back south, news arrived that on 28 September William had landed his army at Pevensey. William proceeded to ravage the local countryside, much of it owned by the Godwines, whilst he awaited the arrival of Harold at Hastings. The two sides met in battle at Senlac on 14 October. Harold had again needed to top up his forces as he marched, and no doubt there were many men from his Sussex estates and his manorial interests in Brighthelmstone who fell on the field that day, alongside their king.

Whilst William took most of his victorious army towards London he sent a smaller detachment through Sussex to take Winchester. On the way they were

William the Conqueror and his knights trample some archers. (Myrabella)

instructed to subdue the local populace and impose Norman authority on this Godwine stronghold. Their route took them to Lewes and then followed the scarp slope of the Downs through Plumpton, Hurstpierpoint and Steyning to Arundel.

The route of this march, and its effects on the surrounding countryside, can be clearly traced in the records from the Domesday Book of 1086, which show a drop in the value of the land that had been laid waste some twenty years previously. The same source shows that the three manors of Brighthelmstone, on the other side of the Downs, fared little better. Two of them were recorded as having fallen in value, from 200 shillings in Edward's time, to 160 shillings after the Conquest. The manor controlled by Harold seems to have come in for special treatment, its value falling from 172 shillings to just 100 shillings in the aftermath of defeat.

By the time of Domesday, the values of all three manors had recovered to 240 shillings, as the new Norman overlord, William de Warenne, sought to improve the profitability of his estate and consolidate his domain.

AD 1264

THE BATTLE OF LEWES

THE VICTORY OF Frenchman Simon de Montfort and his army over that of his brother-in-law, King Henry III, at the Battle of Lewes in 1264 is often seen as a key moment in the birth of English parliamentary democracy. It might also be described as a ruck with the in-laws.

The battle was the first major clash of the 2nd Barons War, in which the barons of England took up arms in response to royal backsliding over treaty obligations. It followed the 1st Barons War some fifty years previously, in which Henry's father King John had sought to evade the conditions that the Magna Carta had imposed upon him.

Simon de Montfort, previously the king's adviser and godfather to his son, the future King Edward I, found himself at the head of a group of rebel barons who were determined to win back their privileges. During the early part of 1264 the respective armies played a game of cat and mouse across the south of England, eventually meeting at Lewes on 14 May. Whilst the Royalist army had slumbered in the town,

Simon's forces had marched from the Weald up to the top of the Downs, to command a position overlooking the town.

De Montfort had been born into military campaigning. As a child he had been at the siege of Toulouse, where his father had met an unpleasant but mercifully quick death, after his skull was crushed by a large rock that had been fired from a medieval siege catapult. His experience was put to good use as he not only took advantage of the higher ground, but also used it to hide from view a significant part of his army that he held in reserve.

ORDER OF BATTLE

In plain sight of the startled royal forces that morning were three divisions of rebels; on the left was a group of recently recruited and poorly equipped untrained Londoners, motivated primarily by their dislike of the king; in the centre was the rebel Earl of Gloucester with his retinue, and on the right Simon's son, Henry de Montfort (so named as a tribute to the king in more agreeable times), commanded another division. Unseen over the brow of the hill was a fourth division commanded by Simon himself.

Facing the Londoners were the royal cavalry under Prince Edward, whilst in the centre were infantry under the king's brother, Richard of Cornwall, the King of Germany. King Henry himself was on the left with his hastily roused force facing his namesake on the rebel side. In all it is estimated that there were 5,000 on the barons' side, and 10,000, including around 3,000 cavalry, under Edward, in the royal army.

Lewes Castle. (charlesdrakew)

LET BATTLE COMMENCE

The battle commenced with Edward's cavalry charging straight into the London division opposite. Edward had a fierce dislike for the Londoners, following an earlier incident in that traditionally rebellious city. Sometime before, his father had taken refuge in the Tower of London from the irate citizenry, who had become tired of having to pay for his various costly schemes. The Queen had tried to join her husband in the Tower, but whether because he suspected a plot by his besiegers, or for more domestic reasons, Henry had refused her entry. This resulted in the unfortunate Queen falling prey to both physical and verbal abuse by the mob, from which she had to be rescued by the Mayor.

The Londoners, with little or no protective clothing, and armed only with a motley assortment of staffs, axes and household utensils, could now see several thousand well-armoured horsemen thundering across the Downs towards them at speed, equipped with lances, maces and broadswords that had their names on them. Not surprisingly, and perhaps according to Simon's plan, they ran as fast as they could, back down the steep slope of the Downs and into the Weald, being pursued and slaughtered all the way by the Royalist cavalry.

Some of the horsemen caught up with the rebel baggage train, which included a caravan that carried de Montfort's banners. In it were locked what must have been something of a rarity for that time, several Royalists from London. They had been brought on the march to prevent them trying to incite the city to turn against the rebels. Edward's knights refused to believe their despairing and impassioned pleas, and they, like so many other of their fellow citizens, met their end at the point of a horse-borne lance or sword.

THE KING RESTORED

A year after Lewes, de Montfort was struggling to maintain his alliance. Many of his former allies had switched sides, and Prince Edward had escaped custody and was leading the rejuvenated royalist forces.

Edward had learnt well from the hard taught lessons of the previous year, and forced Simon and his army into battle at Evesham. The Prince had lured de Montfort onto ground of his own choosing, and trapped the rebel forces in a loop of the River Avon. They were slaughtered to the last man, and after de Montfort had died fighting, his corpse was dismembered, and his head, feet, hands and testicles were hacked off.

THE BATTLE TURNS

Whilst the cavalry were hunting and slaughtering Londoners through the Weald, the remaining two infantry divisions of the king's army were now facing an arduous advance uphill to meet the main body of the baronial forces. As de Montfort's men took the less tiring downhill route to meet them the advantage swung to the rebels, particularly when the previously unseen reserve division was brought into action.

Already exhausted by their exertions, the morale of the king's men was destroyed, and they fled back into town. Leading from the rear was the king's brother Richard of Cornwall, who had tried unsuccessfully to hide in a nearby windmill. To the humiliation of the erstwhile King of Germany, the rebels taunted him with cries of 'Come out, come out, thou wretched miller.'

Much of this phase of the battle took place near Lewes Prison, where around 500 skeletons were found in each of three mass graves uncovered during its construction in 1810. Another mass grave of similar size was found some years later near the Priory of St Pancras, where the king had retreated to as the day turned against him.

Many more bodies would have met a more watery grave, as the royal forces desperately tried to escape through the marshes and across the River Ouse. Most of the Scottish contingent who were fighting on the king's side that day were reported to have had their throats cut by the victorious rebels. One of the few survivors was Robert Bruce, whose grandson, Robert the Bruce, would fight Henry's grandson Edward II at Bannockburn some fifty years later.

As Lewes burned to the ground, set ablaze by the retreating Royalists, the king and his surviving retinue went into captivity.

AD 1554

BURNT TO DEATH
IN A BARREL OF PITCH

BRIGHTON RESIDENT DERYK Carver was the first of the seventeen Lewes Martyrs, put to death by burning for their heresy against the Catholic religion, during the reign of 'Bloody' Queen Mary in the sixteenth century.

He was part of a sizeable Flemish community who had sought asylum in Brighthelmstone, during the Protestant King Edward VI's rule, from the religious persecution they had suffered in Flanders. He owned the Black Lion Brewery, in the street of that name, for some eight years before Mary came to the throne in 1553.

Such had been Deryk's integration into his new homeland that he would regularly hold readings from the English Bible at his home, a practice that was encouraged during Edward's reign. With Mary's accession and her restoration of the Catholic faith, such activities were seen as heretical and became fraught with danger. The Catholic Church was concerned that making the Bible available in English would democratise the word of god and allow individuals to make their own interpretations of the words it contained. Much better if it remained in Latin, to be transmitted according to the strictly defined meanings as reproduced by the priesthood.

So it was that one night his house was raided by Edward Gage, the High Sheriff of Sussex, and all twelve of those present at the Bible reading were scooped up for investigation by the Church authorities. Most were released after recanting their heresy, but Carver and three others kept their faith. For this they were unceremoniously interred in London's Newgate Prison, where they awaited interrogation by the notorious Bishop of London, Edmund Bonner.

Bonner was not averse to rolling up his own sleeves when it came to the work of getting sinners to repent – particularly, it seems, if they were young men. Foxe's *Book of Martyrs* contains a number of accounts of such prisoners being kept in the stocks in the bishop's coal hole, before he beat them with willow and birch twigs. Such was his dedication to the repentance of sinners, he would

*Edmund Bonner –
the bashing Bishop
of London. (John Foxe's*
Book of Martyrs*)*

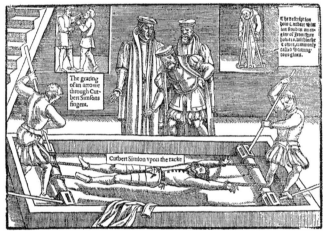

*Near fatal traction.
(John Foxe's* Book
of Martyrs*)*

*Immolation on the
Channel Islands.
(John Foxe's* Book
of Martyrs*)*

whip them until he was too exhausted to carry on, and the very tools of his punishment were falling apart.

Perhaps at the age of 40 Carver was spared such personal attention from the bashing bishop, although it seems likely that he would have been tortured in the attempt to get him to see the error of his ways. Despite his best efforts, Bonner could not get Carver to recant, and he persisted in his heretical beliefs, including his view that the word of god as contained in the scriptures should be freely available to all and sundry. This was a little ironic as in 1539, whilst in Paris as ambassador to France for Henry VIII, Bloody Bonner had supervised the printing of the first official Bible in the English language. Indeed, the Parisian authorities had actually seized some of the pages of that publication on the grounds of heresy.

Whilst Bonner's creeds would prove to be flexible, Carver's faith remained unswerving. He responded to the bishop's final demand to recant by saying: 'If Christ were here you would put Him to a worse death than He was put to before. You say that you can make a God: ye can make a pudding as well. Your ceremonies in the Church, be beggary and poison.' For these beliefs he and two of his group were sentenced to die in the flames of hellfire, which would have prepared them in Bonner's view for an eternity in similar conditions. The three heretics were to have their sentences carried out at different locations in order to serve as a warning to as wide an audience as possible.

Carver was transported to Lewes to await his fate.

Death by burning sounds like a highly unpleasant experience, but apparently for the really unfortunate there were differing degrees of suffering involved. One such example is reported in the Book of Martyrs, where one of three condemned men appears to have been facing the wind, with harrowing consequences:

> Two died without any particular retardation, but Coberly, from the current of wind as he stood, was a long time in perishing. His left arm was visible to the bone, while the right, but little injured, beat upon his breast softly, and the discharge from his mouth was considerable. Rising suddenly erect from hanging over the chain, as if dead, he gave up his mortal abode for one made without hands, eternal in the heavens!

An even worse account concerned the heavily pregnant Perotine Massey, sentenced to death on Guernsey along with her mother and sister. The small mercy of strangulation prior to burning went awry when the rope caught fire and plunged them into the flames. Here the dying Perotine gave birth to a baby boy that was rescued by an onlooker. The bailiff supervising the proceedings instructed that he should be thrown back into the fire to perish alongside his heretical mother.

Deryk Carver's fate was to meet his maker in a flaming barrel of pitch, on 22 July 1555. On his way to the place of

As the example of Bishop Bonner demonstrates, a flexible approach to matters of religion was no bad thing if one wanted to survive in the turbulent times of the Tudors. Another man who survived and indeed prospered in this period was Sir John Gage.

Originally from Surrey, he had risen through the court of Henry VIII to become Chancellor of the Duchy of Lancaster. His Catholicism hadn't prevented him signing the petition to the Pope for Henry's divorce from Catherine of Aragon in 1530. Nor did it stop him from gaining considerable personal wealth and property in Sussex on the dissolution of Battle Abbey. His estates grew when he was awarded some of the lands previously held in the county by Thomas Cromwell, who had met the executioner's axe on Tower Hill.

In 1554, during the reign of the Catholic Queen Mary, he had helped to suppress the Protestant rebellion led by Thomas Wyatt. The Princess Elizabeth was his prisoner in the Tower at this time, and a contemporary author noted that Gage was 'her bitter enemy, but more for love of the Pope than for hate of her person'.

John Gage was perhaps fortunate that he died in 1556, before his former prisoner became queen. His son Edward, who had arrested Deryk Carver, was possibly equally grateful that any such direct personal animosities had passed with his father.

execution, where the present Town Hall now stands in Lewes, the townspeople called out to him and to god to give him the strength to face his ordeal. He knelt down and prayed, then undressed and stepped into the barrel.

His Bible had been thrown into the barrel by the Sheriff, and Carver retrieved it and threw it back into the watching crowd. Despite death threats from the Sheriff, the crowd refused to throw it back into the burning barrel. As the flames licked around him, Deryk Carver's last words were, 'Oh Lord, have mercy on me', before he called out to Jesus and died.

The Marian Persecutions would claim the lives of another sixteen Protestants in Lewes, including ten in one day in June 1557, and some 300 more around the rest of the country, before Mary herself died in 1558.

AD 1651

THE GREAT ESCAPE

SUSSEX WAS LARGELY spared from the ravages of the English Civil War. Most of the gentry of the county had declared for Parliament, reflecting to some extent their dissatisfaction with the rule of Charles I. This was particularly so in the east, where fundamentalist puritanism had taken hold in the towns of Rye, Lewes and Brighton. For most of the population the war was an occasional nuisance, such as when they were volunteered by their landlords to serve on either side, or possibly even worse, when outside troops were in the vicinity, living off their land.

There were some minor skirmishes during the early years of the war, as Royalists from the west made incursions into the county. During the latter part of 1642 there was something of a phoney war going on around Chichester, where forces from both sides were training in close proximity. Eventually Sir Richard Ford took the city for the Crown, and set off into the Weald to try and take Lewes from the north. He had got as far as Haywards Heath before running into Sir William Waller and his

Parliamentary forces, travelling more strongly in the opposite direction. The Roundheads drove the Cavaliers back through Arundel to Chichester, which they captured after an eight-day siege.

The biggest clash of the war came almost a year later, when the Royalist Lord Hopton invaded Sussex from Hampshire, possibly following the route used by Caedwella 1,000 years previously. Arundel Castle was taken by Hopton and he installed 1,000 men there. Waller swiftly raised a force 10,000 strong and on 13 December they besieged the castle. There being a sense of chivalry between the respective nobles in command of each side, the Royalist ladies were allowed out each day to take dinner with Sir William in the Parliamentarian camp. For the menfolk inside the walls there was no such relief and the starving garrison surrendered on 6 January 1644.

Whilst the war would rumble on intermittently for another eight years, Sussex enjoyed relative tranquillity. The last major clash on English soil would be the Battle of Worcester in

September 1651. Here Charles II and his mainly Scottish army were resoundingly defeated by Cromwell's New Model Army. Three thousand Royalists were killed, and 8,000 Scottish prisoners were sent to the colonies under debt bondage. Charles, keen to avoid the fate that befell his beheaded father some two years previously, embarked on an epic escape journey that would see him arrive some 600 miles and six weeks later in West Street, Brighton.

Charles fled Worcester accompanied by two of his senior aides, the Lords Derby and Wilmot, and a sizeable bodyguard. Cromwell had put a bounty of £1,000 on his head and dispatched cavalry units to seek him out. It was decided he would be less conspicuous travelling in a smaller group, so most of the company went in the other direction with Lord Derby, and were shortly after intercepted by Roundheads. Lord Derby was executed. Charles, Wilmot and a few others made their way south towards Bristol, seeking a ship for France.

His flight was assisted by an assortment of Royalist sympathisers, including a network of Catholics who had gained some experience of going underground themselves during the previous 100 years. He would at various times hide from the close pursuit of the Roundheads in priest-holes, rain-sodden woods, the ruins of Stonehenge, and of course in the famous oak tree. His hair was cut and he adopted a range of humble personas to conceal his identity, at one time a woodman, at another a lady's servant. So effective was the disguise that his identity remained a secret, and even one of his own soldiers from Worcester claimed on seeing him that the king was at least three fingers taller.

The search for a vessel proved problematic. At Bristol there were no ships heading to France, so the party headed for the south coast, but their luck didn't improve. Charles and a female sympathiser, Juliana Colingsby, pretended to be a runaway couple seeking passage across the Channel, and had hired the services of the captain of a craft in Charmouth. Unfortunately for the would-be lovers, the captain's wife suspected that her husband was about to get himself into trouble with the authorities. She took a less romantic view and refused to let him take them, locking the skipper in their bedroom to ensure his compliance.

Further up the coast at Southampton another booking was made on a ship bound for France. At the last minute it was commandeered to take troops to the Channel Islands. By now Charles must

It took Charles II ages to grow his hair back. (Library of Congress, LC-US262-38492)

have been doubtful that he would ever get away, and his nerves cannot have been settled by the sight of the villagers at one of his resting places exuberantly celebrating the rumours of his death.

Finally, through the good offices of a supporter in Sussex, Colonel Gunter, a passage was arranged on board a coal ship that was in Shoreham Harbour, owned by a Captain Tattersall. It was arranged that the fugitives would meet the skipper at the George Inn, on West Street. They left Hambledon on the night of 13 October and set off across the Downs to Brighton, hoping that this time their plan would come together.

There weren't many Parliament troops left in Sussex at this time, but the escapees succeeded in finding them. As they passed near to Arundel Castle they crossed paths with Captain Morley, the governor, and some of his troopers, but the fugitives held their nerve and walked past them. They had a similar close shave at Bramber, where a squadron of troops had recently been stationed to guard the bridge. By the time they saw the Roundheads they themselves had also been spotted. Fighting the urge to turn and run, they rode unchallenged past the guards, who were fortunately few in number as most of their comrades had adjourned to a nearby hostelry.

They had ridden but a few miles further when they heard the thudding of galloping hooves coming up behind them, and their spirits dropped as they saw the forty Roundhead cavalry from Bramber fast closing in on them. Charles, Wilmot and Gunter slowed down and stepped aside, their hearts in their mouths, so near to sanctuary and yet so far. Their pursuers showed no signs of stopping, and to their great relief the cavalry rode past them at speed, blinded to their real target in their haste to attend to a false sighting.

Shortly after, Gunter rode down to Shoreham to check on arrangements, whilst the other two went over the Downs through Portslade to Brighton, arriving on the night of 15 October. They met up again at the George Inn on West Street where they sought shelter, refreshment and quite possibly, given their recent experiences, a change of underwear. Here they met Captain Tattersall for the first time, who had agreed a fee of £80 to transport what he understood to be a man fleeing following the fallout from a duel.

There would be one final heart-stopping twist in this tale. Having successfully hidden the king's identity from the searching Roundheads and even a member of his own guard, he was finally recognised by the drunken landlord of the George Inn, Anthony Smith. On seeing Charles he took his hand and, kissing it, said: 'It shall not be said that I have not kissed the best man's hand in England.' Fortunately for the fugitives it could not be said that he gave them away. Whilst Smith's loyalty knew no price, that of Tattersall required a further £200, once he realised the identity and value of his cargo.

This was money well spent, and at 2 a.m. on the morning of 16 October, Charles set sail for the Continent, where he would spend the next nine years. Shortly after their departure, government cavalry arrived in Shoreham, having just missed their prey yet again.

After the Restoration, Tattersall was given a pension, and his coal-brig was renamed the *Royal Escape* and made a ship of the line, surviving until it was broken up for fuel in 1791. Smith the landlord had neither sought nor received any further reward. Tattersall for his part jealously guarded his role in the great escape, and always resented Smith's somewhat less mercenary contribution. Some twenty years later Tattersall was still using his position to malign Smith over parochial matters in Brighton.

Charles II left a longer-lasting legacy to Sussex in the form of his direct descendants, the Dukes of Richmond.

This was the fourth creation of the Dukedom and it was awarded to Charles Lennox, the illegitimate offspring from a dalliance with the Duchess of Portsmouth. Lennox bought what is now the family seat at Goodwood, in West Sussex, in 1697. Subsequent generations have added to the original Jacobean house and estate, including that essential feature for luxury living, one of the finest race-courses in the world.

Livius wins the 2.15 at Goodwood Racecourse. (Steve Cargill)

WHO NEEDS PARLIAMENT ANYWAY?

Perhaps not surprisingly, Charles II enjoyed an on/off relationship with Parliament after his restoration in 1660. He suspended sittings on numerous occasions when he disagreed with the direction it was taking, and if that didn't work he simply dissolved it. There were four parliaments during his reign, and he dissolved all of them, and decided to do without their inconvenience for the last four years of his reign.

Much of the dissatisfaction in the later parliaments revolved around the introduction of the Exclusion Bill, which sought to keep Catholics, and in particular his brother James, off the throne. Despite his considerable ability to father children out of wedlock, legitimate heirs were less forthcoming, hence the concerns over James.

It was during this period that the modern political shape of the nation took form, growing from the religious divisions of the preceding 100 years and the more recent splits of the Civil War. The group pushing for the exclusion of James became known as the Whigs. They stood for constitutional monarchy but against absolute rule and the Catholic tendencies of those who promoted it, as well as those Stuarts who would benefit from it.

On the other side were the Tories, named after Irish outlaws, who wanted a strong monarchy and were in dread of anything that sniffed of republicanism. From these roots came the Liberal and Conservative parties that we know today, with the Labour Party joining them over 200 years later in 1900.

AD 1703

STORM WARNING

BRIGHTON HAS FACED many dangers throughout its history, but none have been as persistent and unrelenting as that posed by the waves that wash up on its shoreline. The risks were particularly severe when many of the fishermen and their families lived in houses on the beach, in what was known as the Lower Town. The whole area was flooded in 1340, and again in 1665 when a violent tempest washed away the shops and cottages of lower Brighton.

The best record of these early storms is to be found in Daniel Defoe's account of the Great Storm of 1703. This blew in off the Atlantic across large swathes of England, leaving death and destruction in its wake. Defoe collated records of the night from around the country, providing one of the earliest and most complete records of such a weather-related event.

As the storm came ashore at Shoreham that town was flattened and the ruins were visible for many years afterwards. Brighton was next to be hit as around 1 a.m. the winds blew in at hurricane force, taking the roofs from houses and stripping the lead from the tops of churches. Several windmills stood no chance against the gales, which levelled them to the ground. As the light of dawn revealed the full extent of the damage, the town looked as though it had been bombarded by cannon overnight.

Such was the power of the wind that vegetation was salted at considerable distances inland. Twenty miles from the coast near Ticehurst, a doctor, for reasons best known to himself, chewed on the leaves of a hedge and found them to be salty. On hearing of this, women in Lewes discovered that their unpicked grapes had been similarly seasoned.

Waves ... (Tanay Sharma)

Wind ... (DJB)

Even the sheep on the Downs were reluctant to eat the grass, and when forced to do so by hunger, their shepherds reported that they 'drank like fishes' afterwards.

ALL AT SEA

For all the destruction on land, it was to be at sea that the town suffered its greatest losses. The fishing fleet travelled far and wide along the British coast to fill its nets, and when the storm blew in many were not able to make it to a safe haven. Some boats – the lucky ones – were blown out of control across the North Sea. Having lost their anchors, sails and masts they ended up as far away as Holland and Hamburg.

Less fortunate were the crew of the ketch the *Richard and Rose of Brighthelmston*, lost with all hands off the coastal village of St Helens. Most of the crew of the *Richard and Benjamin*, stranded off Chichester, survived by clinging onto the ropes at the top of the mast. They were luckier than those aboard HMS *Newcastle*, which went down nearby with the loss of more than 200 men.

The *Elizabeth* and the *Happy Entrance* would never return to Brighton, both sinking to the bottom of the North Sea. They took all on board with them, bar a sole survivor, Walter Street, who spent three days riding the waves and hanging on to the top of the mast for dear life, before he was finally rescued near Great Yarmouth.

Several other vessels and crew members were lost in what must have been both a human tragedy and an economic disaster for the town, with its already declining population heavily reliant on the fishing industry. Two years later a more localised, but equally destructive storm finally destroyed what remained of the Lower Town, the ruins of which may still lie buried beneath the pebbles of the present-day beach.

As Brighton enjoyed a renaissance sparked by Dr Russell's water cure, the town took steps to protect itself from the sea and erected further groynes on the beach. These served to largely protect the town from the worst of the previous disasters, although the Chain Pier, built beyond such protection, would suffer on numerous occasions during the nineteenth century, until it finally succumbed to the elements in 1896. Another great storm in 1850 was reported to have had thunder like bomb shells and incessant lightning before it moved on down the coast.

Neptune had a bit of a breather until the summer of 1929, when a 20ft-high tidal wave surged up the beach, causing the crowds of holidaymakers to run for their lives. Their deckchairs and possessions

STRANDED ON THE GOODWIN SANDS

One of the most horrific episodes of the Great Storm of 1703 occurred on the Goodwin Sands, a sandbank just off the coast of Kent. Legend has it that in Saxon times it was an island owned by the Godwineson family, which had been taken over by the waves, now only to surface at low tide.

On the night of the storm four large ships of the line from His Majesty's Navy, along with many other smaller civilian vessels, were washed up on or near the sands. Here many hundreds of men who had survived the initial tempest had sought refuge from the cauldron of the surrounding seas. It was only a temporary respite, however, as the men knew that soon the tide would rise and engulf them once again.

Despite their awful situation, visible through looking glasses from the land, the only boats that came out from nearby Deal were seeking to salvage goods and chattels, not the bereft men. Even the coastguard vessels refused to put to sea, despite the pleas of the town's Mayor, Thomas Powell.

An outraged Powell called the townspeople together and offered a share in 5 shillings per head for each man that could be rescued. Several volunteers came forward and boats were commandeered from both the lacklustre coastguard and the salvage hunters. They managed to rescue 200 men before the tide reclaimed the sands and provided a watery grave for the hundreds still left behind.

The good Mayor then had to pay out of his own pocket for both the upkeep of the rescued men and their eventual transport to the navy yard at Gravesend. The Queen's Agent for Sick and Wounded Seamen had refused to provide even a penny to their cause, as he hadn't received any orders to do so!

According to naval records there were 253 men on board HMS *Northumberland* and 386 on HMS *Restoration*. None survived. Only one man survived from the *Mary*'s complement of 273, by swimming from wreck to wreck until he reached the *Stirling Castle*. From this last vessel some seventy men (out of 349) are recorded as having been rescued.

The difference between the naval figures for those rescued, and Powell's total, may indicate that a significant number of those who survived might have quite understandably lost their sea legs, and deserted to the safer life of a landlubber. Alternatively, some of the rescuers may have been seeking to bump up their bounty.

Pool Valley in the storm of 1850. (Reproduced with the kind permission of the Royal Pavilion and Museums: Brighton and Hove)

Sussex coast storm damage – the hurricane of 1987. (Phil Sellens)

were left bobbing up and down behind them. Several days later the body of a young woman, who had been bathing when the wave arrived, was washed up beneath the cliffs at Rottingdean.

The most recent clash with the elements was the Great Storm of 1987, the largest since 1703, when 100mph winds battered their way across southern England. Nineteen people died, four of them in Sussex.

Dutch Elm disease had killed 10 million trees in the ten years that preceded the storm, although Brighton, protected by the Downs and the sea, had escaped infection and was home to the largest surviving collection in Britain. There was no escape from the winds that blew in that night, however, and the town took its share of the 15 million trees that were toppled in the space of six hours.

Pebbles from the beach were whipped against the windows of seafront houses, a minaret crashed through the ceiling of the Pavilion, and at a site in Peacehaven it was a miracle that no one was killed as 200 caravans were thrown through the air.

With sea levels rising and climate change generating ever more unsettled weather, it is only a matter of time before the next Great Storm hits.

AD 1795–1800

CORRUPTION IN THE CAMPS

AT THE END of the eighteenth century Brighton had all the appearances of a garrison town, with thousands of soldiers camped nearby, to guard the Regent (and the town) from any surprise attacks that might be launched by the revolutionaries across the Channel. The British military establishment was slowly modernising in response to the French threat, and not a moment too soon if the following tales of corruption in the higher ranks of the Militia regiments were anything to go by.

In early March, 1800, the camp of the Hampshire Fencibles cavalry regiment at Brighton was rocked by a financial scandal. The paymaster, Lt Hunt, had apparently done a runner with £6,000 worth of regimental property, including £900 that he had withdrawn from two banks in town. It was reported that he had embarked on a waiting vessel at Rottingdean, and left his wife behind. In a related development the head of the regiment, Col Everitt, had ordered the arrest of his deputy, Lt-Col Dacre, and charged him with embezzling money intended for the troops.

After three weeks under close arrest, Dacre was brought before a court martial, and a somewhat different story emerged. He claimed that the paymaster had been unable to issue any money to him, as £1,500 had already been improperly loaned to Col Everitt from regimental funds. Dacre had repeatedly asked permission to pursue Hunt to London whence he had fled (by road), but Everitt refused him each time.

'But he went that way – to London.'
(Lobsterthermidor)

By the end of the trial the finger of suspicion was pointing firmly at Everitt as having bribed his paymaster to flee, taking with him all proof of his own financial misdemeanours. Rumours abounded in the camp to such an extent that a small group of junior officers wrote a letter to him, which was published in *The Times*. They expressed their concern at the 'false and infamous insinuations and assertions which are hourly propagated to injure your character.' It might have carried a little more weight had a few more of their brother officers felt concerned enough about their colonel's tattered reputation to join them in signing it. Here, this story, like the disbanding Hampshire Fencibles, disappears from the pages of history.

Of greater permanence in the annals of military misdemeanour was the case five years previously, featuring John Fenton Cawthorne, colonel of the Westminster Regiment of the Middlesex Militia. Cawthorne's criminality was quite extraordinary, even by the admittedly low standards of the time. For him this was not the age of universal enlightenment, it was the era of his enrichment. He treated the regiment as his own private revenue stream, and the wellbeing of his men and the defence of the realm would not be allowed to get in the way of this primary mission.

Despite his many failings being continuously reported to his superiors and several near mutinies, he repeatedly escaped censure until his outrageous behaviour was brought unavoidably into the public eye, during the court martial of one of his officers at Brighton Camp in July 1795. As a result of evidence

The Middlesex Militia in 1799; after Cawthorne was court-martialled they were fully staffed, fully equipped and fully clothed. (DJB)

CORRUPTION RETURNS TO THE COMMONS

It will probably come as no surprise to discover that someone with Cawthorne's innate desire to enrich himself at the public's expense, whilst expending a minimum of effort, was also a Member of Parliament. He had been expelled from the House following his military misunderstanding, but he would eventually return as the slightly less than honourable member for Lancaster.

In September 1819, with the nation still in shock from the reform rallies of that year, which had culminated in the Peterloo Massacre, the local worthies in Lancaster had gathered to make a declaration to express their outrage at such seditious activities. The final passage spoke of 'our determination to enforce the due execution of the laws against all who incite the ignorant to acts of violence, and thereby endanger the peace and security of this realm.' The proposer was Cawthorne.

He had perhaps forgotten his first attempt to seek re-election in that place, after his ban was lifted in 1802. He had already been canvassing on behalf of a certain Col Bowes who was standing for a civic position, before he threw himself into his own election campaign. In the closely contested poll, where the major issue was that of his still odious reputation, he lost to the two candidates standing against him on an anti-corruption platform. There was a record turnout, including over 700 new voters who had registered in the run-up to polling day.

When the results were announced, the new MPs, the Marquis of Douglas and John Dent, were chaired through the streets by a cheering populace. The banners that preceded them carried messages proclaiming 'The Honour of Lancaster Preserved', 'Integrity and Honour Triumphant' and 'Independence and Virtue'.

As the joyous procession passed the unsuccessful candidate's house, his mob of disappointed supporters proceeded to attack it with rocks and stones. Several of the townspeople were severely injured before the attackers were chased away, and the outraged citizens went back to Cawthorne's house and smashed all of his windows.

By hook, or more likely by crook, Cawthorne would eventually regain his seat in Parliament, and held it until he died in 1832, bequeathing his widow a series of cases in the debtors courts that would occupy her for the next five years.

---

produced at that hearing, the colonel faced his own court martial at Horse Guards later in the year, on fourteen separate charges. In thirteen of them, he was found guilty of behaving 'in a scandalous infamous Manner, unbecoming the Character of an Officer and a Gentleman', and 'CASHIERED, and declared unworthy of serving His Majesty in any Military Capacity whatever'.

Space precludes a full consideration of Cawthorne's misdeeds, although for the dedicated legal scholar the 400 plus pages of the proceedings of his trial are still in print today in what has become a standard text, over 200 years later. For present purposes a résumé of one of his favourite cons will suffice to give a flavour of his greed, avarice and corruption.

The militia men were recruited by ballot in their home counties, and frequently those so chosen, known as principals, could if they had the financial means provide a substitute to serve for them. In the Westminster Regiment the system was finessed so that the principals paid a sum of money, and left the regiment to use that payment as a bounty to encourage a substitute to enlist. Whilst this mechanism was not unusual, the economics as practised by Cawthorne were. The principals had to pay 12 guineas (or more) to avoid service, whilst the recruiters were instructed to pay no more than 8 guineas in bounty to recruit substitutes.

Not content with this 4 guinea top-slice, when signing on, the recruits had to sign or mark a form that had in very small print (for those who could read), if at all, a section saying that the bounty paid included 1 guinea for clothing and one more for the marching payment. These were both separately funded grants that the government paid to the regiment. Thus for each substitute soldier the regiment recruited it showed a 6 guinea profit, which went into the colonel's private account. It couldn't get much better than this.

Well, yes it could. If they didn't actually bother to recruit a substitute, then Cawthorne could double his money and trouser the full 12 guineas. This he did with great frequency. At the trial it was established that only one in three of the principals who had paid to

avoid service were actually substituted. Falsified numerical returns gave the appearance of normality, and kept the allowances coming in. On closer scrutiny it turned out that the regiment had never been less than eighty men short of its establishment of around 550.

Mathematicians will say that you can't get more than 100 per cent out of something, despite what present-day football managers might tell you. They obviously hadn't met Cawthorne. He was already running a series of scams charging men who wanted to be discharged, and also those who had deserted and then been recaptured. If a deserter could pay up, he had merely been on leave; if not, he received between 500 and 700 lashes.

The corrupt colonel wanted not just the milk and cream from his cash cow, he wanted jam with it. In perhaps his finest fiddle, he was paid money at both ends of the transaction. He sold sixteen of his best men to an old colleague, Lt-Col Bowes, in another regiment, the Durham Fencibles, for 20 guineas a head. He then replaced some of them with deserters who had also paid to return to the regiment.

For the Middlesex Militia, under-manned, underpaid and underequipped as they were, their one piece of good fortune was that they never had their weaknesses exposed in battle whilst encamped at Brighton and Shoreham.

AD 1795–1936

GAMBLING MANIA

IN 1806 A correspondent for *The Times* wrote that 'at Brighton, such is the mania for gambling, that everything becomes the subject of a wager'. He wasn't joking. Numerous reports from the period suggest that betting on just about anything was hard-wired into the DNA of the town, perhaps not surprising given the influx of the idle rich with both time and money to spare.

An early example of this was the wager struck in 1795 by the diminutive Sir John Lade with the more portly Lord Cholmondeley, that he could carry him on his back twice around the Steine. At the due time Sir John instructed the corpulent Cholmondeley to strip, as he had bet on carrying just his Lordship, and not his clothes. It was perhaps best for the dignity of all concerned that the bet was conceded without having to be tested.

In contrast to the 'Starkers Steeplechase', the wager struck between two officers of the Light Dragoons in 1801 seemed positively normal. One cavalryman had to draw a light carriage, known as a gig, the 6 miles

between Brighton and Lewes in under four hours, whilst the other had to cover the same journey in reverse. The first officer arrived in Lewes with an hour to spare, but the one pulling to Brighton ran into severe difficulty on Falmer Hill. Spectators thought his challenge was over, but revitalised by brandy and water, he found his second wind and arrived in Brighton to collect his 20 guineas prize with two minutes to spare.

Several years later, one late September evening in 1804, a large crowd had gathered on the beach and the cliffs above to observe what had been widely advertised as the spectacle of a man walking on the water. Not surprisingly they were disappointed. Equally unsurprising was the apology that was pasted up on North Street the following day, which stated that 'this liberty was taken with the public in consequence of a wager.'

Much of the gambling during this period took place in the libraries, which followed the gentry into the town. In these establishments the call of 'place your bets please' was far more likely to be

Playing dice in a library, by Thomas Rowlandson. (Dcoetzee)

heard than the present-day requests for silence. In addition to reading materials and the taking of refreshments, there was much demand for the gaming opportunities offered within. Loo, a card game, was very popular with the ladies, whilst the gentlemen were noisily crowded around the hazard tables throwing dice.

The local magistrates, as arbiters of what was right and proper, were particularly concerned with the danger of gambling where the moral welfare of women was concerned, and sought to have the game of Loo banned. After several unsuccessful attempts, the killjoys of the bench eventually succeeded in banning all gaming in the libraries, after Walker's Library, a perpetual thorn in the side of the authorities, had allegedly fleeced a foreign visitor of £300 at the rouge et noir card table. Several local papers

questioned the motives behind the ban in 1817, upsetting the Chief Magistrate Mr Sergeant Runnington, who felt that there had been a gross misrepresentation of the facts. But it was to no avail, and stripped of this important revenue stream the libraries soon declined.

Gambling also occurred under less scrutiny in private accommodation, sometimes hosted by unscrupulous parties who had followed the gentry and their riches into town. In 1800 Sir Thomas Southcott claimed to have been a victim of such individuals after he lost £6,000 at cards, blaming his bad fortune on the fact that his fellow players had got him drunk. Unable to pay up he fled Brighton but was apprehended on the road to London by his creditors, and placed in custody. The judge that heard the case sympathised with the baronet, and ruled that the debt be dismissed.

A similar tale was told some twenty years later by a Mr Comber, described by *The Times* as 'a young man of great respectability'. He claimed that a professional gambler by the name of Collins had invited him round to supper, following which considerable drinking had ensued. On waking the following morning his host informed Comber that they had played hazard long into the early hours, and that he now owed him £243. This came as something of a surprise to Comber, as he claimed he didn't even know how to play the game. Again the judge found in favour of the respectable debtor, and saved him from having to pay up.

Whilst there is no doubt that there were some criminal elements who would use drink to prepare their victims before taking their money, it seems that the widespread acceptance that such practices went on provided a ready excuse for those upper-crust losers who were just rubbish at gambling. This was particularly so when the judges invariably took the side of those wealthy enough to be of 'good character'.

Even winners could be losers, as one London businessman found to his cost in 1802, after winning £50 from a professional dice player. The pro was probably setting up his mark by allowing him to win a bit at first, before taking him to the

GANG WARFARE

Misbehaviour at racecourses continued into the twentieth century, with the notorious razor gangs of the inter-war period fighting for control of the lucrative bookmaking business. This was most famously represented in the film *Brighton Rock*, with a vicious fight at Brighton races being the centrepiece. This scene was actually based on an incident that occurred at the now closed Lewes Racecourse in 1936.

A gang of thirty Londoners had arrived, armed with hammers, crowbars, billiard cues, knuckledusters and a hatchet, and attacked rival bookmakers Alfred Solomon and Mark Frater. Despite being hit on the head, Solomon managed to get away. Frater was less fortunate, and was held by the arms by one Londoner, whilst another hit him with the hatchet. On falling to the ground he was repeatedly kicked, punched and beaten by the rest of the gang before they attempted to flee from the police, dropping their weapons as they went.

Brighton policeman DC James arrested a man by the name of Mack and told him that he had been involved in the attack. 'Not me, guv'nor,' responded Mack as he tried to run away. In all, sixteen members of the gang were arrested.

At the ensuing trial Solomon and Frater suffered an understandable collective amnesia regarding the events of that day, whilst the defence lawyers argued that the police had made mistaken identities on all of the suspects. This did not prevent the judge handing down stiff sentences to those convicted for the assaults. This was to be the last major outbreak of gang violence on British racecourses.

Brighton Racecourse in the nineteenth century. (Reproduced with the kind permission of the Royal Pavilion and Museums: Brighton and Hove)

cleaners. He was therefore a little put out when the supposed victim picked up his winnings and tried to leave. The punter was also a little put out, with force through a glass window, sustaining a pair of black eyes and a badly cut shoulder in the process.

Of course no review of gambling would be complete without touching on the sport of kings (or indeed regents), horse racing. Regular meetings were held at both Brighton and Lewes, well attended by all levels of society, and patronised by the Regent and his aristocratic friends. Betting was an integral part of the sport, and it may surprise present-day punters to learn that 'betting in-play', that is once a race has started, was not unusual at

these events. It would be some 200 years before online betting exchanges re-introduced this mode of separating punters from their cash.

The considerable sums being wagered also attracted the wrong sort of people at the other end of the social scale, including swindling bookies known as blacklegs and the ubiquitous pickpockets. Good order was frequently maintained by the powerful presence of 'Townsend and Sayers', two men who ran an early private security operation. So successful were they in their business, and so impressed was the Regent, that within a few years they were providing a personal bodyguard service to the royal family.

AD 1803–1827

PISTOLS AT DAWN

AS WE HAVE already seen, the town's infatuation with gambling could frequently end in tears. In keeping with the latter-day chivalry of the Regency period, arguments of a sporting nature could often be resolved by recourse to a sporting solution, that of duelling, most frequently with pistols.

Such events were not uncommon in this period, and the 'debt of honour' that led to them was usually a more mundane debt of money that had accrued after a hard night at the gaming tables. Despite repeated attempts, such contests rarely ended with any of the participants even sustaining a wound, never mind a fatal injury. This is perhaps no surprise given that they had been drinking all night long. Their drunken state thus made them more likely to resort to such an extreme method of resolving their differences, whilst at the same time ensuring that they were unlikely to come to any real harm.

Following one such dispute over a game of cards in 1806, the Earl of Barrymore and a Mr Howorth proceeded at four o'clock on a Friday morning to the vicinity of Block Bottom, between Brighton and Rottingdean, to settle their differences. Having fired a case of pistols each with no success, their seconds intervened and, possibly realising that it might take hours until one of the duellists sobered up enough to score a hit, declared it a no contest.

This would probably have upset the assembled company of gamblers who had accompanied the duellists to Block Bottom, and had bet heavily on the outcome of the duel. The Earl of Barrymore may well have been relieved to survive, as he was the rank outsider

Duelling pistols. (Daderot)

and odds of 7/2 were being offered about his chances of winning!

A few years earlier in 1803 in a similar incident at Whitehawk Hill, two officers from the South Gloucester Militia sought to resolve a mess-hall argument from the night before at sunrise. It took three exchanges of fire before one of these trained military professionals could even find their target, and having winged his opponent, honour was declared satisfied by the seconds.

In 1811, a Mr P and a Mr M had fallen out over the dice at a hazard table, and trod the by now well-worn early morning path to the east of Brighton to resolve the issue. What then transpired remains a mystery, but they returned the best of friends some eight hours later, presumably having spent longer at lunch than at the pistols.

The location of these duels to the east of Brighton might be seen as suggesting that the west of the town, or Hove, had already acquired the reputation for gentility that still persists to the present day. However, a simpler explanation for this geographical cluster lies in the fact that they were seeking to catch the sun rising in the east at dawn, in order to see what they were doing. Given the diffi- culty of aiming through beer goggles, it is debatable as to how much difference this actually made.

Duelling with pistols might in fact have been a safer way to resolve disa- greements than indulging in the ancient method of having a good old-fashioned punch up. The only fatality that resulted from a gaming-related argument was the

'Why don't you stand a bit closer, you might hit me?' (DJB)

result of fists, not flintlocks. A dispute over a game of cards in the Richmond Arms led to a fracas that started in the pub and was then taken outside on the instructions of the landlord. On arrival at a nearby field the instigator of the trouble, James Launder, told his opponent James Gale, 'I'll kill you before you go.' It didn't quite work out like that and Gale got only a one-month sentence for the manslaughter of Launder, from a judge sympathetic to his justification of self-defence.

It should not be assumed that duelling with pistols was the exclusive resort of the upper classes. Following an argument in a pub, bricklayer Daniel Perren took issue with builder George Cheeseman over some comments he had made, and wrote him the following letter:

Sir,- As you last night Accused me of lying and Idleness and Insulted me on the Score of Poverty I feel myself aggrieved you are a good shot at a

Pigeon or Sparrow I therefore request you will Provide a Pair of pistols and a second, and Meet me and mine at 5 o'clock In the Morning near Upper Wick Pond. I am Sir Yours D. PERREN. P.S. let me know If you accept the challenge.

Cheeseman took the matter to court, where, despite much amusement at the letter, the magistrate remanded Perren in custody.

A more serious example of the use of a duel as a device to bully and intimidate is to be found in the records of a court case of 1827. This involved the complaints of Morris Barrow, a lawyer resident at 25 New Steine, about the 'disorderly' activities being carried on by the women who were the new tenants next door. They had set up a brothel to coincide with the summer season.

Barrow told the court that he had seen hundreds of men, including the local vicar, entering the premises and that sometimes business was so brisk that the carriages of the clientele were queuing round the square. Relations with the neighbours went steadily downhill, particularly when they failed to draw the blinds whilst entertaining.

The antagonism reached its peak just before the end of the season. Some officers of the 52nd Regiment of Foot, who had been among the best regulars at No. 24 and were perhaps suffering from the anticipated frustration of the imminent closure of the premises, took out the said frustrations on Mr Barrow and his family.

Having threatened him with a horsewhipping several nights before, they returned and broke his windows. In the process they accused his wife and daughter of being whores, and demanded the satisfaction of their somewhat dubious honour through a duel. Barrow, expecting trouble, had invited two local constables to be on hand, and they promptly arrested the officers and charged them with riotous assembly.

When the case of the brothel came to court, both the presiding judge and the prosecution were less than ardent in their pursuit of the case against the ladies concerned, perhaps taken in by their apparent charm and innocence. Alternatively it could be suggested that they had, along with the vicar, been enjoying the charms of the ladies themselves.

The case was thrown out as was that against the soldiers, and the ladies moved on to the next focus of the social calendar. Meanwhile, life in the New Steine returned to normality and Mr Barrow no longer needed to worry about being able to find a parking space for his coach in front of his house.

AD 1801–1834

STAND AND DELIVER

THE POPULAR IMAGE of highway robbery during the eighteenth and nineteenth centuries involves the largely fictional activities of Dick Turpin, still being romanticised in recent times by the likes of Adam and the Ants. The reality was of course more complicated, and coaches on the roads to Brighton saw many attempted robberies by a variety of means, some more successful than others.

The traditional rural hold-up remained a favourite amongst some sections of the criminal fraternity, although it tended to focus on private carriages, which were softer targets than the larger coaches with up to fourteen passengers on board. However, one gang, who specialised in urban snatches, didn't even wait for the coach to leave London, cutting the straps holding the trunks in place whilst it was still on Blackfriars Bridge.

More typical of the overt robbery was a case in 1826, when a Mr and Mrs Pagham were travelling home to Eastbourne in their carriage, along a

dark country lane. Three Brighton-based ruffians ambushed them with clubs and a struggle ensued. Mrs Pagham received a punch in the face that had been intended for her husband, who had ducked. She was dragged to the ground and threatened with violence as her husband lashed out at the man holding the reins. The horses ran free and Mr Pagham, perhaps demonstrating where his priorities lay, chased after them whilst his wife screamed for mercy from the men demanding her money.

Having retrieved the carriage (and perhaps his courage), Mr Pagham set upon the assailants, shouting that 'they should either have his life or he would have theirs'. This unsettled the erstwhile highwaymen and they ran back to Brighton, where they were arrested the following morning.

A few years later a Mr Mason and his friend were similarly ambushed on the Brighton Road near Croydon. Mason cracked the whip and the horses ran over one of the villains, as the other pulled his pistol, fired, and missed the fortunate Mason. Mason then fired back in return, wounding one of the robbers and causing them both to flee. Having reloaded his pistols he chased them into some nearby woods where they disappeared.

Perhaps more familiar to the present-day reader, street robbery was also a hazard of the period. One night a waiter was walking home down St James's Street in Kemptown, when he was accosted by three strangers who asked him the time. Their next request was for his money, but they had to settle for his watch. All three were apprehended shortly after, tried and sentenced to death.

More successful than these somewhat desperate physical attacks were what might be termed 'stealth robberies', which frequently involved considerable sums of money and were only discovered after the felon had disappeared over the horizon with the loot.

In an early example of such a theft, £3,000 being transferred between banks was stolen from the 'secure' box inside the London to Brighton coach in 1812. The money had been locked, Russian doll-style, in a tin that was then locked in an iron chest, which itself was locked in a cupboard under a seat, the keys for which were held by the bankers at either end of the journey.

On arrival in Brighton the tin was found to be as open as it was empty. The inside of the coach was equally bereft of the four passengers who had been aboard when it left London. A man and woman had got off at Mitcham when it was claimed that she was ill, whilst the other two men had alighted at Reigate,

Standing room only on the outside of the Brighton coach. (Reproduced with the kind permission of the Royal Pavilion and Museums: Brighton and Hove)

stating that they had business to attend to before they would complete their journey to Brighton the following day. They, like the money, never made it to Brighton, and they, with the money, were last heard of in Blackfriars, enjoying a good supper.

Presumably in response to such thefts, the coach companies moved their locked-box facility from inside the coach to under the driver's seat. So it probably came as something of a surprise when a Brighton banker opened the still-locked box on the arrival of the coach from Southampton, to find no trace of the expected £1,000 that had been deposited in it by a colleague in Worthing. On closer examination the box seemed undamaged, with the exception of one small screw that was loose.

The coach had started with thirteen passengers, and arrived in Brighton with six still on board. The finger of suspicion pointed at two outside passengers who had dismounted at a pub near Shoreham, to meet a friend. The driver

This passenger didn't want to wait for the driver to sober up. (DJB)

had disappeared into the pub for about five minutes, purportedly to organise some change for the fares, but perhaps equally likely to seek refreshment.

The police arrested Thomas Hollingshead in connection with the robbery and took him to court, but neither the driver nor the stableman at the inn recognised him as being involved. He was, however, picked out of an identity parade by the guard of the York Express, as having been on board when a large sum of money went missing from that coach. The guard, however, became suddenly unavailable to testify, and the case crumbled.

Robbery was not the only danger to visit those travelling by coach. In 1834, the 65-year-old Mr Richards, who was Lord Gage's Land Agent, sued the *Brighton Gazette* for libel. The paper had printed a story regarding Richards' 'ruffianly behaviour' towards a married woman and her daughter. In a scenario that will resonate with many women who have travelled on a crowded underground train, he had rubbed up against them, and more, whilst they were travelling on the Lewes coach.

After another female passenger had accused him of being a 'dirty old fellow', the coach was stopped and he was made to sit on the outside. On arrival at Lewes he had to flee to the Star Inn to escape the anger of those present. The jury awarded him damages of one farthing.

Travelling on the outside could also make for a hazardous journey, particularly if the coach suffered one of the not infrequent accidents. One Brighton-bound coach was crossing London Bridge when it crashed, sending one unfortunate external passenger on to the road with such force that his brains came out of his ears!

Within a few years such hazardous transportation became a thing of the past, as the London to Brighton Railway opened in 1841. The golden age of highway robbery was over, the new era of train robberies had just begun.

'Where's the RAC when you need them?' (DJB)

ONE LAW FOR THE RICH ...

The satirical Czech author Jaroslav Hasek, in his classic short story *The Criminal's Strike*, wrote of how if the rich were caught stealing it was classed as kleptomania, whilst the poor were treated as nothing but common thieves.

He might as well have been referring to the sentencing system in England in the early part of the nineteenth century. On Boxing Day 1822, a boy of 14 years of age was tried for stealing a gold watch from a jeweller's shop in Brighton. On being confronted by the shop owner he had burst into tears and returned the timepiece. He was found guilty of theft by the jury, and the judge sentenced him to death.

Almost three years later a young man was in the same court for exactly the same crime in the same place. The difference between the two was that this thief was 'of respectable appearance and of good connexions in London', and able to call upon witnesses to his good character from infancy. This did not stop the jury from finding him guilty, but the prosecutor urged clemency due to his background, and he escaped without any serious punishment.

The sentencing priorities of the judges also look a little inconsistent to the present-day eye. Transportation to the new colonies on the other side of the world had become the in-vogue punishment; Australia was Britain's Siberia. At the 1829 winter assizes in Lewes, a man was found guilty of stealing some stockings, riband, lace and money from the Brighton drapers where he worked. The thief was transported for life.

At the same assizes a man was convicted of killing a young woman on the Old Steine. He had beaten her several times on the head, and she died from the concussion caused by those blows. The killer was sentenced to transportation for seven years.

If you were very lucky, you might get a couple of years on the treadmill. (Reproduced with the kind permission of the Royal Pavilion and Museums: Brighton and Hove)

AD 1817

THE BATTLE OF THE TAR TUB

IN THE EARLY nineteenth century Guy Fawkes night was a traditional time of celebration on the Old Steine at Brighton. For this one night of the year the ordinary people of the town would participate in a lively and well lubricated evening of suitably themed entertainment. This featured fireworks of many descriptions and built up to the centrepiece of the festivities, the rolling of a flaming barrel of tar.

In 1817, the High Constable of Brighton, John Williams, had decided to scale down these somewhat chaotic proceedings, and had summoned all of the town's quasi police force, known as headboroughs, to be on duty that night. His reasons for doing this are obscure, and whether it was due to an early concern for health and safety, or perhaps out of respect for the Prince Regent, whose mother was in the terminal stages of an illness, remains a mystery.

Perhaps he just didn't like seeing the wrong sort of people enjoying themselves, on what was effectively the Regent's front yard. Whatever his motives, his actions on that night divided the town and resulted in a series of riots over the next few days in which it was a miracle that only one person died.

At around sunset on Wednesday, 5 November 1817, a crowd of around 200, mainly boys, had gathered at the Steine, and in common with previous years were amusing themselves with an assortment of squibs, serpents and fire-crackers. The trouble started at around 9 p.m. when a procession of people arrived with a flaming tub of tar at their head. This was the appointed time for the police to swing into action.

A fierce tussle ensued to gain ownership of the blazing barrel, and eventually the forces of law and order

The Olde Steine in more normal times.
(Reproduced with the kind permission of the
Royal Pavilion and Museums: Brighton and Hove)

were successful. They extinguished the flames in the tar tub, but these actions ignited a fire in the growing crowd. The High Constable's hose, the High Constable himself, and then his house to which he had retreated, came under attack from the crowd. His officers were forced to withdraw under a hail of stones and anything else that came to hand.

As he was writing messages to call out the Magistrate and the military, a rock came flying through his window. Several companies of the 21st Fusiliers were roused from their beds, where they had been resting after having only just marched into town that morning. No doubt tired and irritable, they proceeded with fixed bayonets and effectively kettled the Steine, and awaited further orders.

By 9.30 p.m., the disturbances had grown to the point where Sergeant Runnington, the town Magistrate, was forced to read the Riot Act, his recital being regularly punctuated by the sound of heavy rocks landing in his vicinity.

The soldiers were by now also receiving the attention of the crowd, and several squibs had been lobbed in their direction. With the urging of the town officials in their ears, a section of soldiers reluctantly made their way forward to apprehend the culprits. In the melee that ensued one of the head-boroughs, John Rowles, was stabbed in the back by a bayonet. It was done with such force that it detached from the musket and went straight through him, leaving 3in of the blade protruding from his stomach. He was carried home

'Call out the guard!' (DJB)

where he endured in agony until he died the following night.

As the clashes continued there were a number of other serious injuries. Miss Wymark of New Street was lucky to survive being shot in the head, whilst two of the 21st Fusiliers, Burt and the appropriately named Slaughter, were seriously wounded by the hail of rocks. It would be 3 a.m. the following day before the rest of their by now exhausted comrades could return to their barracks and their beds.

At some point under the cover of all this chaos there was some score-settling going on as well. A local revenue officer by the name of Redmore was spotted by James Bennett, an operator of small carriages known as fly-by-night machines. Redmore had recently given evidence against Bennett, who had also been operating an illicit shop selling spirits.

Bennett, his wife, and several other friends had pursued the unfortunate Redmore across town, pelting him with

'Ere soldier, can I 'ave me squib back?' (DJB)

mud, rotten eggs and less pleasant projectiles, and threatening to kill him. He was chased out of several houses in which he had tried to gain sanctuary, on one occasion being dragged out by his hair. When this case came to court some six months later, Redmore was still too ill (or perhaps frightened) to come and give evidence in person.

The following day, in a show of defiance, a large crowd again gathered on the Steine, and let off the last of their fireworks, undisturbed by officialdom, before retiring peacefully to their homes. On the Friday evening, however, the crowds were back out, with intent to cause damage to the property of the two men most associated with the mishandling of events two nights previously, Williams the High Constable and James White, the local rate collector. Both

houses were particularly vulnerable as all of the police officers were attending the Coroner's Court inquiry into the death of their colleague John Rowles.

White's house in Castle Square was the first target at around 9 p.m., and forty panes of glass were shattered under a barrage of bricks and rocks. The crowd were temporarily subdued by the conciliatory words of a local man, Mr Newbold, but then they attacked Williams' property just up the road. Within a few minutes another sixty window panes had been smashed, and worse was being threatened when the local vicar, the Revd R.J. Carr, stepped in to address the mob. His words had a more permanently calming effect on the crowd, and they dispersed for the night.

Rumours abounded of plans for similar destruction the next day, and extra security arrangements were made. The Magistrate ordered what was effectively a curfew, when he sent out a circular to the masters of houses and to housekeepers, warning them to keep all servants and dependents indoors after sunset. All remained quiet on the streets, but dissatisfaction over the handling of the situation continued in the courts.

Most of the town felt that the attempt to curtail and then control the Gunpowder Plot celebrations had been an unnecessary and tragic mistake. At the locally convened Coroner's Court inquest in the week that followed, the jurors expressed their unhappiness at the actions of the town's officials. They brought a verdict of 'wilful murder' against a soldier, Private James Day, and of 'aiding, abetting and comforting the said James Day', against Williams and White. A town meeting convened at the Old Ship Hotel heard many more complaints about the measures that had been taken.

The authorities fought back, and sought to censure in the courts the editor of the *Brighton Herald*, W.M. Fleet, who was summonsed for printing details of the events of the 5th that might influence potential jurors against Williams and White. Fleet defended his publication on the grounds that it was a true and accurate record, with discretion taken in the naming of those responsible. Whilst this may seem a rather novel and naïve approach to the jaded newspaper reader of the twenty-first century, such things were important 200 years ago. Not to the judges, however, who backed Williams and White, and found the case against the editor. However, 'in the interests of the peace and tranquillity of the place whence it came', they declared the matter should be dropped.

The case for murder finally came before the Sussex Assizes in Horsham some four months later. Whilst Private Day was in the dock, *The Times* reported that Williams and White 'who were men of very respectable appearance were exempted from this ignominious ceremony.' All three were found not guilty of what the judge deemed to be an accident, on the technicality that the coroner's inquest had not stated that the death of Rowles was due to the wound caused by Day's bayonet!

Less fortunate, although by the standards of the times relatively leniently treated, was James Bennett, who was given a two-year prison sentence for his part in the riot. In this case the judiciary were no doubt trying to re-assert the importance of law and order, without stirring up further trouble in Brighton.

FIREWORKS AT LEWES

The world-famous bonfire night celebrations at Lewes were not always the harmless fun which today attracts so many visitors.

In the early nineteenth century, as in Brighton, they were an opportunity for the ordinary people to come out and let their hair down for one night a year. The culmination of such anarchic celebrations was in 1847, when, after the reading of the Riot Act, the military and the police fought a long drawn-out battle with the Lewes Bonfire Boys.

Following the carnage of that night the present-day Bonfire Societies were founded, transforming the festivities into what historian John Lowerson has described as 'controlled popular effervescence'.

AD 1831

TRUNK MURDER PART I

ONE OF THE most notorious events in nineteenth-century Brighton was the murder of Celia Holloway by her husband John. What made this case stand out from the numerous other killings that the town has seen was the manner in which John Holloway disposed of the unfortunate Celia's body. In both respects he was assisted by his other wife, Ann Kennett.

Holloway had met Celia some six years previously when he was nineteen and she was twenty-five. She had soon become pregnant. When he denied all responsibility for her condition she returned to her home village of Ardingly, where she applied for parish relief. There the local administrators used the bastardy law to have Holloway incarcerated for failing to meet his parental responsibilities, and offered him financial encouragement to marry Celia. No doubt this short-term investment would be considerably cheaper for the parish in the long run.

Eventually Holloway accepted these inducements, but the marriage soon descended into acrimony and violence.

Celia was removed from the matrimonial home by her brother, along with the furniture for which he gave her errant husband £2. Holloway went away to sea, returning to live in Brighton, some years later, with a second wife, Ann Kennett. Following a brief reconciliation, Celia, now pregnant again by Holloway, applied in April 1831 for an order to make him pay maintenance of 2s a week. Their first child had died as an infant.

When he failed to make the required payments on time, Holloway was visited at his work on the Chain Pier by the district Overseer, who threatened to bring him before the bench if he didn't resume them. He promptly went round to Celia's lodgings to remonstrate with her. He shouted: 'Madam, you think you are going to frighten me, but you are mistaken – you damned bitch, you shall suffer for this before many days.' At this point the landlord stepped in and gave Holloway his marching orders. As he was leaving he made a parting shot: 'You don't know as much about me as a great many, or you would mind your Ps and Qs.'

*The Chain Pier, where John Holloway worked.
(Reproduced with the kind permission of the
Royal Pavilion and Museums: Brighton and Hove)*

A few days later Ann Kennett was sent round with just 1s for Celia. She wasn't too impressed and made her feelings clear. 'Is that all you have brought me? I have nothing to eat – what am I to do with one shilling? I will go [to] the overseer, to know which John is to keep – his wife or his whore.' Having vented her anger in words, she now grabbed a poker and hit Ann with it several times. Kennett restrained her and with not a little restraint on her own part, informed Celia that, 'You are too little to hit – but mind, you shall suffer for this.'

These would prove to be no idle threats, as John was now plotting to reduce his family responsibilities. On several nights he invited Celia out, but she was rightly suspicious of his intentions and refused to go with him. John developed his plan; he would now pretend to reconcile with her and then kill her at their new home.

On the morning of 14 July he came round and collected her belongings and took them to a house he had rented the previous day, on North Steine Row (aka Donkey Row). He returned that afternoon to pick up a tearful Celia, who despite his rough treatment had been worried that he wouldn't come back for her as promised.

She would find to her cost that Holloway was keeping Ann's earlier promise that she would suffer. As they entered the new lodgings John followed Celia up a few stairs and made to kiss her. Instead he pulled out a rope and proceeded to strangle her. In the struggle they fell down the stairs, Celia hitting her nose on the way. Holloway, unable to finish his victim on his own, ordered the hiding Ann Kennett to assist him. With her help Celia was quickly subdued, and possibly still alive, hung by the rope from a nail in the coal cupboard under the stairs. If she wasn't already dead, this would have killed her.

Holloway, a former butcher's boy, had planned to dismember the body for easier disposal, but decided to wait a while in order that the blood might congeal and provide less evidence of their acts. As Holloway and Kennett left for their home on Margaret Street, they took with them Celia's clothing, which they had already sorted into two piles, one for the pawn-brokers and the other for the hearth.

The following day they returned to the scene of the crime and proceeded to dismember the corpse, the blood now having become more like jelly. The head, the arms and the legs were wrapped in a bed cover and dumped that night in the communal privy behind Margaret Street, with Kennett following Holloway to make sure no blood was leaking out.

The main part of the body and the detached thighs were loaded into Celia's trunk and placed onto a borrowed barrow. This was pushed through town by Holloway, whilst Kennett followed with a pickaxe and shovel wrapped in a parcel. On reaching the Hare and Hounds they turned left towards New England Farm and headed for a copse known as Lover's Walk. On arrival they found it was too dark to carry out their task, so they returned at dawn the following morning to complete their grisly mission. The ground was inter-woven by numerous tree roots, so they buried the body parts as best they could, before breaking up the box and disposing of it nearby.

After they had cleaned up the murder scene and left Margaret Street for new lodgings on nearby High Street, they might have thought they had got away with it. Unbeknown to them, events that would lead to their arrest were already unfolding, albeit in a peculiar fashion. Some ten days after the burial, a labourer had noticed some disturbed ground whilst walking in the wood, and on closer inspection found a piece of cloth. He looked no closer, but mentioned it to his wife on returning home, who suggested that it might have been a buried child.

Displaying an apparently remarkable lack of curiosity, he made no further investigation but continued to mention the matter to people in passing conver-sations. It was several weeks before a return visit was made to the site and after a woman's dress and an awful smell were uncovered, a constable was called for.

The torso and thighs were discovered and the police investigation moved rapidly, with Holloway and Kennett taken into custody the following day. A lengthy search of the privy at Margaret Street eventually uncovered the remaining parts of the body. An autopsy revealed that it was technically a double murder: the stress of the attack had induced labour and the top of the baby's head was visible.

By the time the murder case came before the Lewes Assizes in December, Holloway had made a series of contra-dictory confessions. All professed his own guilt, but alternated between implicating and exonerating Kennett. A procession of witnesses testified to the guilt of Holloway and the assistance of Kennett.

John Holloway was without doubt a bully, with women and children his preferred victims. By his own confession he had raped several women and possibly murdered another. Both of the women in this case were in fear of him and had suffered previously at his hands. His attitude to children became clear during the trial, during his fierce cross-examinations of them after they had given their testimony. Despite his worst efforts the brave youngsters faced him unflinchingly, refusing to be cowed into changing their evidence.

As he was being led to the dock one day a 10-year-old boy had said, 'That's Holloway, I know his voice.' Holloway looked at the boy fiercely before punching him hard between the eyes, blacking them both and bruising his young face; 'It is Holloway and you will remember him,' he added.

In addition to his bullying ways Holloway was also subject to severe mood swings. He was at times profoundly depressed, and tried to kill himself on several occasions in prison. At other times he displayed confidence in abundance, which verged on arrogance during the trial. He had also managed to organise a conspiracy whilst incarcerated, persuading some of the worst elements to join him in a plot to murder the guards and the governor and then escape. The plan fell through when it was revealed by a young surgeon who was doing time for bigamy.

There was to be no escape for John Holloway. He was found guilty of wilful murder and sentenced to death by hanging. A few days later, on 16 December, he met his maker at the end of a rope, in front of a large crowd at Horsham Jail. Ann Kennett escaped the noose having been found not guilty of murder, and walked free in March 1832, with her newly born child, having got away with the charge of aiding and abetting.

The year 1831 was not a good one for women in Brighton. In a postscript to the Holloway case that has the hallmarks of a copycat killing, in early December a young woman by the name of Hannah Hobbs was discovered floating just offshore. Her arms had been cut off and her head was almost completely severed. No one was ever charged with her murder.

THE TIMES PRINTS A RETRACTION

On Thursday, 28 August *The Times* had reported with some distaste that the woman now residing in the house where the murder and subsequent dismemberment took place was earning good money by showing visitors around the premises. Perhaps cognisant of its future role as the 'newspaper of record', the accuracy of its reporting was of great importance.

The following week, upon receiving new information regarding the grim tours, *The Times* carried a correction to its original report. It was the journalistic equivalent of the token award of a farthing's damages in a libel case:

> It is not true, as our Thursday's contemporary has stated, that the woman who lives at No. 11 Donkey Row, 'is reaping a rich harvest by showing the wretched and dreary looking hole.' The habitation is, beyond question, properly described; but the very civil and industrious people who reside in it have not been indemnified at scarcely more than one penny per hour for the time they have consumed in answering the questions and gratifying the curiosity, of their numerous visitors.

AD 1216–1860

THE FRENCH

FOR MILLENNIA, THE Sussex coast has been a favourite point of entry for would-be invaders and raiders. None have been as persistent, regular and dedicated in such missions as our near neighbours, the French. Between 1202 and 1815 the English (and after 1707 the British) went to war with France no less than twenty-two times, including the Hundred Years War that occupied most of the period between 1337 and 1453. Every century from the thirteenth to the nineteenth was marked by at least one and usually more conflicts.

Ironically the earliest and the most successful incursion was during a period of peace between the states, and occurred in 1216, when Prince Louis of France was invited over by barons rebelling against King John. He landed in Kent and marched with his army to London, where he was proclaimed King of England at St Paul's Cathedral. King John had fled to Winchester, from where he was soon evicted by the all-conquering Louis.

With John's death later that year the perfidious barons started to switch their allegiances back to the newly crowned Henry III, and Louis headed to France for reinforcements. Unfortunately for Louis his route took him through Sussex, where the locals proved inhospitable, ambushing him near Lewes and bottling up the remainder of his force at Winchelsea, from where it was lucky to escape.

In 1377, during the Hundred Years War and whilst peace negotiations to end the conflict were on-going, the French Navy spent the summer raiding along the south coast. Rye and Hastings had been burnt to the ground before the fleet arrived at Rottingdean and a large force of men was landed. They proceeded to pillage the village before setting it alight. Local legend has it that a large number of the villagers had sought sanctuary in the tower of St Margaret's Church, and up to 100 perished there in the flames.

A force of around 500 men had been mustered by the Prior of Lewes to see off the invaders, and they marched to the beleaguered village. The French commander, Jean de Vienne, aware of their approach, had prepared an

The French raid of 1514. (Reproduced with the kind permission of the Royal Pavilion and Museums: Brighton and Hove)

ambush using his cavalry. In the ensuing skirmish, 200 Englishmen were killed, whilst the Prior of Lewes and several knights were captured and taken back to France to be ransomed.

In June 1514, Henry VIII was negotiating a treaty with France, to end a war that had been as successful on the battlefield as it had been disastrous for his treasury. Whilst there was talk of peace in the air, from across the water came another French raiding party. This time their target was Brighton, where they landed, looted and then lit the whole town ablaze, burning it to the ground.

Henry was a little peeved at this action, and responded by sending the appropriately named Sir John Wallop with 800 men across the Channel to seek retribution. Whilst in Normandy

they destroyed twenty-one villages, two harbours and a large number of ships. The peace treaty was signed a month later. Perhaps the only positive to be taken from this episode is that it inspired the earliest plan of Brighton that survives today, an illustration of the town ablaze as French ships lie offshore.

Some thirty years later, it was another war with France, and more peace talks. The French launched an attack on the English coast to strengthen their position in getting Henry to give up his last two English possessions in France, Calais and Boulogne. The attack fell largely and unsuccessfully on the Isle of Wight and the Solent, where the *Mary Rose* sank during the battle.

The French fleet then sailed east looking for targets of opportunity.

Above *'Keep rowing* mes amis, *only another 125km and we'll be in Brighton.' (DJB)*

Right *Napoleon taking a geography lesson – 'You go to Dieppe, turn left and England's in front of you.' (DJB)*

As they neared Brighton the local population had responded to the alarm beacons and chased away the few that landed there. A more significant landing was made at Seaford, but that place having little of interest to them, they soon departed back home.

Perhaps one of the most significant clashes in Anglo-French warfare, in a long history that includes Agincourt, Blenheim, Trafalgar and Waterloo, was the less famous Battle of Beachy Head, in 1690. On the seas off the Sussex coast a French fleet resoundingly defeated a combined Anglo-Dutch force, sinking eleven ships in the process.

In the aftermath of this humiliating defeat it was decided to vastly increase the size of the Royal Navy, but William III had a credit rating lower than that of present-day Cyprus, and no funds. So he set up the Bank of England. Using the funds so raised the fleet was rapidly expanded, providing a considerable stimulus to the then embryonic Industrial Revolution.

The victory at Beachy Head gave the French a short-lived period of control over the English Channel, with knock-on effects for those on its margins. The Brighton fishing fleet had considerable difficulty in pursuing its livelihood, under the ever-present danger posed by the warships. In 1694 six French vessels appeared off Brighton, so close to the shore that their cannon shots were missing the town and flying over the rooftops and into the fields behind. A rapid muster of the townsfolk discouraged the French from making a landing and they sailed away.

The eighteenth century marked a new low point in relations between the two kingdoms as they expanded imperiously across the globe, finding new and exotic locations in which to carry on their feud. Back home in Brighton, Anthony Relhan, author of one of the earliest histories of the town in 1761, used the pen as his weapon against the French. In a marvellous demonstration of retro-spective xenophobia, he suggested that the English Druids found in Brighton in pre-Roman times were of course 'more knowing than those of Gaul, more strict in observing, and more punctual in adhering to their original institutions.'

As France underwent the convulsions of the Revolution, it made little difference to relations with Britain. The Revolutionary Wars morphed seamlessly into the Napoleonic Wars, with a brief interval before the final act at Waterloo.

Brighton had a particularly active year in 1796. In January a French ship ran aground in very rough conditions near the town, and to the amazement of the locals around 230 English prisoners came ashore in a very bedraggled state. The people of Brighton had a

BRIGHTON'S INNKEEPERS – THE LAST LINE OF DEFENCE?

In 1804, whilst the threat of Napoleonic invasion was concentrating British minds, *The Times* drew attention to the poor state of defences on the Sussex coast. There was but one frigate and only thirty cannon in all the batteries between Shoreham and Eastbourne to hold the French at bay. The local fishing boats provided a good early warning screen, 'but far more formidable are the Brighton Innkeepers, who would send the French packing with just one bill!'

The enterprising nature of the local inhabitants had already been noted some years previously, when in 1793 the annual Brighton Camp had been extended due to fear of the activities of the revolutionary Sans Cullotes. The unhappy officers, having already broken down their accommodation in preparation for departure, found themselves having to rebuy all their doors and floors from the gleeful Brightonians, who had already collected and recycled them.

In 1812, as Napoleon was fighting his way towards Moscow, one British officer was having his own battle against the proprietor of the Castle Inn. He had been shocked at the size of his account and took the matter to court. The magistrate found in his favour and reduced the bill, noting that 'some of the people of Brighton not only fleeced but also skinned their visitors'.

Shoreham Redoubt – built to calm recurring doubts about our new allies. (kennerton)

whip-round to provide them with food, clothing and shelter before they were sent on to reception camps. One spring morning the town awoke to the sound of cannon fire but were helpless to do anything to prevent the capture of a British sloop by a French privateer. Fortunes were reversed that autumn as two privateers were captured by the Royal Navy.

Perhaps the most exciting encounter of the year came in November, involving an even more traditional activity than fighting the French, that of co-oper-ating with them in the smuggling industry. An unflagged ship was seen pursuing a smuggler's vessel, and firing on it. Some shots landed near the West Fort, a defensive structure built above the beach.

Grateful for the rare opportunity to get some action, the West Fort battery returned fire on the anonymous ship, which promptly ran up its British colours. This diversion gave the smugglers time to offload their cargo onto smaller craft which then landed on the beach before the coastguard could catch them.

After Waterloo, the next time that Britain and France went to war they were remarkably on the same side, fighting together with the Turks against the Russians far away on the Crimean Peninsula. Perhaps less remarkable was the persistent fear in Britain of invasion by their erstwhile allies, led by Napoleon III.

Whilst the charging Light Brigade and the Thin Red Line were fighting alongside French Cuirassiers in Russia, a somewhat thicker line of concrete and stone was being constructed on the Sussex coast. Littlehampton Fort, Shoreham Redoubt and Newhaven Fort were constructed during the 1850s, and serve as a visible reminder of the persistent fear of invasion from across the English Channel.

AD 1916

'THE DAY THAT SUSSEX DIED'

WHEN ASKED ABOUT the First World War, most people will remember the Battle of the Somme in 1916. On its opening day, 1 July, the British Army suffered its highest ever casualty figures, with nearly 20,000 men killed and a further 40,000 wounded.

Less well known, yet equally brutal, is the story of the diversionary 'raid' on a German salient at Richebourg l'Avoue, some 30 miles to the north, the day before. Shaped like a boar's head this projection into the Allied lines allowed the Germans to rain fire into the British trenches at will, and was seen as a logical point to launch one of a number of diversionary attacks prior to the big one on the Somme.

The attack was carried out by the 116th Brigade, which was comprised of the 11th, 12th and 13th (South Downs) Battalions of the Royal Sussex Regiment. They were known as the South Downs Brigade, having been recruited primarily from the men of that part of the county. These 'pals' battalions were also called Lowther's Lambs, after Lt-Col Claude Lowther, the local MP who had raised them as part of Kitchener's Army.

Whilst there were Brightonians in all three units, they were most strongly represented in the 13th Battalion. They had arrived in France in March 1916, and had been put into the line several times where they soon sustained minor casualties as they became familiar with the wide assortment of weapons that the Germans were using against them.

Despite discomforts ranging from underground mining through to the aerial assault by minenwerfer, barrels of explosive launched from the German lines that would wobble through the air before hopefully landing somewhere else, it was, in the context of what was to come, a relatively gentle introduction to trench warfare.

This would change a few months later as they were moved in June to prepare for the attack on the Boar's Head. Unlike the still green and pristine countryside associated with the start of the Battle of the Somme, Richebourg had been largely destroyed in previous fighting in 1914 and again in 1915, when the

Stretcher bearers at Brighton Station, 1918. (Reproduced with the kind permission of the Royal Pavilion and Museums: Brighton and Hove)

2nd and 5th Battalions of the Royal Sussex Regiment had been involved. It was into this already destroyed landscape that the soldiers of 1916 re-carved their trenches and strongpoints, occasionally exposing the bleached remains of previous incumbents and unspent munitions as they went.

The original plan was for the 11th Battalion to lead the assault, accompanied on their right by the men of the 12th. The 13th was to be held in reserve to provide support and supplies to the lead units. However, on seeing the plans the commander of the 11th, Lt-Col Grisewood, was concerned that too much was being expected of his untested troops, who had been given only days to prepare in the training area, where a replica of the ground to be fought over had been prepared.

Rather courageously, and with some foresight, he informed his superior, 'I am not sacrificing my men as cannon fodder.' Such an attitude could not be tolerated and he was told to 'clear off at once'. The brigade commander, concerned that such defeatism could

have spread into the men of the 11th Battalion, decided to move them into the reserve, and moved the unlucky 13th into the direct assault.

Having spent an extra day in their jump-off positions, following a delay of twenty-four hours in the main assault at the Somme, the first wave of the South Downs pals finally went over the top at 3.05 a.m. on 30 June. The attack was no surprise to the waiting Germans. They frequently made signs to display messages to their opposite numbers across no-man's land: it was in this way the British troops on the front line had become aware of Kitchener's death. Of greater concern were the signs that read 'When are you coming over Tommy?' that had been spotted by the British officers through their trench periscopes.

There had been a preliminary but ineffective bombardment of the German lines, which had left much of the wire in front of their positions intact. When this lifted it was the signal for the Germans to come out of their protective bunkers and set their sights on the British lines. Artillery shells were now landing in the British trenches where the later assault waves were waiting, and those who had already gone over were subjected to a withering combination of bullets and bombs. Most of the men carrying bridges to cross pre-identified obstacles were shot down before they got to them. To make matters worse, new obstacles were discovered that had not been replicated on the training ground.

In those areas where the men had been able to cross no-man's land with some success, an additional complication was provided by the smokescreen that was supposed to cover their advance from enemy eyes. This had drifted back and shrouded the attackers themselves, leaving them unable to see where they were going or where their comrades were. As a result a series of small un-coordinated and fierce exchanges occurred in the German trenches, as bombs, bullets and bayonets took a savage toll.

War poet Edmund Blunden, serving with the 11th, described the horror of such fighting as recounted to him by Sgt Compton, who had seen a German crawling round the corner of a trench. 'I threw a bomb in, it hit the trench side and rolled just under his head: he looked down to see what it was –'.

Company Sergeant Major Nelson Carter was awarded a posthumous Victoria Cross for his role in taking a machine-gun post armed only with a revolver. He then used the machine gun

to cover the retreat of his men before joining them back in the British lines. From there he repeatedly went back out into no-man's land to retrieve wounded comrades. On his final such mission he was killed by a sniper.

In addition to the VC, as a result of their actions on this day soldiers of the South Downs Brigade were awarded a Distinguished Service Order, eight Distinguished Conduct Medals, four Military Crosses and twenty Military Medals. Such a list provides some measure of the ferocity of the fighting and the bravery of the men doing it.

A more poignant indication is provided by the casualty figures sustained in the battle. Three hundred and sixty-six of Lowther's Lambs were killed trying to take the Boar's Head, and more than 1,000 were wounded or taken prisoner. The 12th Battalion suffered 429 killed or wounded in the attack, and even the 11th in its support role sustained 116 casualties. It was the unfortunate 13th Battalion, last-minute replacements in the assault, that suffered most heavily. Around 800 of its men were killed, wounded or captured.

Whilst Brighton and Eastbourne suffered the heaviest death toll at the Boar's Head, historian Paul Reed has suggested that up to 100 other communities in Sussex also lost men. It is little wonder that the battle at Richebourg on 30 June 1916 has come to be known as 'the day that Sussex died'.

WOUNDED INDIANS RECOVER IN BRIGHTON

During the first years of the war Brighton became a treatment centre for thousands of Indian troops who had been wounded on the Western Front. Their accommodation ranged from the luxurious surroundings of the Royal Pavilion and the Dome to the less salubrious confines of the old workhouse on Elm Grove, renamed The Kitchener Indian Hospital.

A decision not to use Indian troops in France led to the closure of the facilities in 1916, but the link to those brave men is maintained at the Chattri War Memorial, on the Downs just to the north of Brighton.

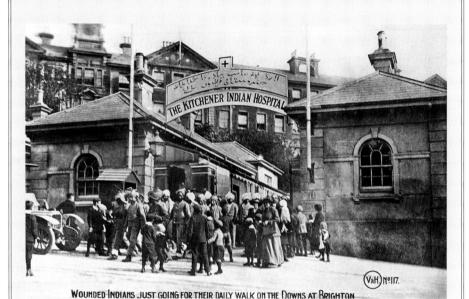

WOUNDED INDIANS JUST GOING FOR THEIR DAILY WALK ON THE DOWNS AT BRIGHTON

Locals and patients mingle at the Kitchener Indian Hospital on Elm Grove. (Reproduced with the kind permission of the Royal Pavilion and Museums: Brighton and Hove)

AD 1915–1918

DEATH IN THE DESERT

PRIVATE **WILLIAM GREEN** of Lowther Road, Brighton, was a career soldier. He had joined up in 1900 to fight in the Boer War, after which he served in India until he arrived at Basra in modern Iraq, with the 6th Indian Division under the command of Major General Charles Townshend. Their primary mission was to safeguard the oil refinery and pipeline at the port of Abadan on the Persian Gulf, vital to Britain's naval interests, from the Turks of the Ottoman Empire.

The overall commander in Basra was General Nixon, described by one psychologist of the military mind as a man 'who made up in ambition for what he lacked in intelligence'. Nixon had more adventurous ideas as to how to deploy his new division, and ordered the ill-equipped Townshend to push north towards Baghdad. After some initial successes they were forced to retreat to the small town of Kut, at which point Townshend decided to make a stand and await the arrival of reinforcements.

By now the division was down to 13,000 men, having suffered 7,000 casualties in the previous fighting. Here, at the start of December 1915, they were rapidly surrounded by the superior numbers of the Ottoman forces, and the five-month-long siege of Kut began.

Several unsuccessful attempts were made by the British to break through to Kut from Basra, but the only soldiers to be relieved were a succession of generals, of their commands. The bitter fighting on these relief expeditions against the well-organised Ottoman Army cost a further 23,000 casualties, nearly twice the number of increasingly hungry men that remained holed up in Kut.

William Green recalled that for the starving men even sleep provided no respite from their hunger. 'When we slept we always dreamed of food, of

Turkish cavalry surround Kut. (Takabeg)

Turkish infantry surround Kut. (Raspar)

tables laden with real banquets – meat, fish, fowl, fruit. And just as we were going to eat it it would disappear and we would wake up.'

By February the Turks had started sending a plane over to bomb the defenders, an early raid scoring a direct hit on the British hospital, killing thirty-two already sick and wounded men. The Royal Flying Corps also started dropping supplies, although quite how crucial the mailbags of letters for the staff officers were remains debatable.

The now desperate British command resorted to a range of previously unthinkable solutions to the crisis. Lawrence of Arabia was part of a secret mission to purchase the relief of the 6th Division for the sum of £2 million, but Enver Pasha, the Turkish commander, turned the offer down flat. The British even asked the Russians for help, and General Baratov and his force of 20,000 Cossacks headed from Persia to Baghdad.

However, following the failure of a boatload of supplies to break through the Ottoman circle, Townshend surren-

dered the town on 29 April 1916, and Baratov and the Cossacks returned to Persia.

What was described as the most abject capitulation in British military history was only the start of the worst chapter in this episode for the ordinary soldiers like Private Green. For a brief moment the officers and the other ranks shared the grim hungry reality of the surrender, in the forbidding shape of the Turkish army-issue biscuit.

Lieutenant H. Bishop described them thus: 'These biscuits need only be once seen or eaten never to be forgotten. They are of a dark-brown colour, unless mouldy, about 6in in diameter and 1in thick in the centre, and made from a very coarse meal, which must contain anything except wheat. They are even harder than the hardest of our own army biscuits.' Fortunately for the lieutenant, the officers were able to purchase a range of additional foods to supplement and replace such coarse fare.

For the ordinary men there were no such extras. The starving William Green traded his greatcoat with a Turkish soldier in return for a couple of the biscuits. He froze at night but at least there was something in his belly. After several days there was an official ration of five biscuits issued. They normally required soaking in water to make them palatable, a process that caused them to expand. Quite a few of the men couldn't wait and consumed them dry, a mistake that some of them lived to regret, as the biscuits painfully expanded in their digestive systems.

The officers also enjoyed a reasonably comfortable journey back to Turkey, at first on barges and then on a variety of equine beasts of burden. There was some concern when the expected two animals per officer were reduced to one, as this meant that once their baggage was loaded they would have to walk. Fortunately they were able to hire extra animals at Tikrit, using the month's wages that the Turkish authorities had kindly paid all the captured officers, in gold. As Bishop recalled, with some sympathy for the men who they had left behind: 'We had survived wonderfully well, and had fared infinitely better than the troops from Kut, who were marching along in our tracks a few days behind us.'

For William Green and the other ranks the 700-mile march, on foot across the desert, was a nightmare journey made on the verge of starvation and exhaustion. Many collapsed along the way, and if they failed to respond to beatings from the guards they were stripped and left to die. Green told the *Brighton Herald*: 'I think you could follow our route by the bits of khaki uniform and by the bones of dead men.'

The column halted at Batchi, where the men were put to hard labour on the construction of a railway line. Possessing nothing more than the sackcloth and rags they were now clothed in, the men slaved for several months on this project, barely sustained by a meagre ration of food. Under such conditions sickness stalked the prisoners, and soon an outbreak of cholera was claiming twenty

Enver Pasha – he didn't take the money. (Gorup)

lives a day. There had been 242 men in Green's regiment as they marched out of Kut and into captivity. By the time they left Batchi there were eighty-seven left.

Green was fortunate to be sent to a hospital in Adana where he recuperated under the care of Armenian nurses, themselves lucky survivors of the genocide that claimed so many of their compatriots. He was then sent to a camp near Constantinople where the hard labour and floggings continued.

It was here that he had perhaps his luckiest escape, when he knocked out a Turkish officer who had slapped him for sitting down whilst at work. Fully expecting to be shot for such conduct, Green was amazed when the officer was ordered to apologise to him. Then, after thirty months in captivity, came the news that the war was over, and after nineteen years overseas Private William Green finally returned to Brighton.

HARD TO SWALLOW

Indigestible army biscuits were not only bringing dietary misery to the prisoners of war in Turkey. On the same day that the *Brighton Herald* ran Private Green's account of life in captivity, tough biscuits also featured in a military story closer to home.

Thousands of veterans were still awaiting demobilisation after the end of the war, and were understandably keen to get home. Over 7,000 men based at Shoreham Camp had refused to parade and instead marched along the seafront to Brighton Town Hall, to register their protest with the Lord Mayor himself.

One particular concern of the soldiers was the fact that they were receiving no bread in their rations: 'They had only hard Army biscuit so hard that you break your teeth on it. Why, they demanded, should civilians have bread and soldiers only biscuit?'

The Mayor, no doubt a little concerned at the sudden appearance of an army of thousands of disgruntled squaddies on his doorstep, duly appeared on the balcony overlooking the now packed Bartholomew's Square, and gave his audience what they wanted to hear, hoping that they would leave his town in as good order as they had arrived. This amounted to a great deal of sympathy, not a little empathy, and the promise of a few phone calls. He had, he told the assembled throng, already phoned the Camp Commandant and arranged for a good hot meal to be provided for them at the camp at 2.30 p.m., upon their orderly return.

As the men marched back to camp, their cheers still ringing in his ears, the Mayor received a concerned telephone call from Winston Churchill, who promised that he would send a special representative to investigate the trouble. Whether this was with a view to dealing with the men's grievances, or with the men presenting the grievances, the *Brighton Herald* offered no opinion.

Turkish soldiers trying out their newly captured weapons. (Takabeg)

AD 1926

THE BATTLE
OF LEWES ROAD

ABOUT ONCE EVERY century, the authorities who run Brighton have had to resort to force in order to demonstrate the importance of law and order to the populace at large. The Battle of Lewes Road during the General Strike of 1926 was one such example.

Following a humiliating climb-down to the coal miners in 1925, Stanley Baldwin's Conservative government made preparations to ensure that it was ready for any industrial action the following year. The Ministry of Health sent a circular out to all Local Authorities advising them to make preparations to maintain services during any such disputes, including the recruitment of suitable special constables. In Brighton a Local Emergency Committee was created in early 1926, formed of five eminent Conservative council members.

A parallel national volunteer body, the Organisation for the Maintenance of Supplies, was also set up, its membership containing a large number of those on the political right. The *Daily Express* had likened the OMS to the Ku Klux Klan and Mussolini's Blackshirts, and even the Commissioner of the Metropolitan Police considered it to be a fascist group. At the start of April the OMS opened an office on Grand Parade, seeking volunteers to maintain public order and no doubt hoping to recruit amongst the large community of fascists in the town at that time.

At the end of April, with a new bout of unrest unfolding at the coal mines, the king signed the Emergency Powers Act and the gloves came off. In Brighton the council's Emergency Committee created a Volunteers Service Committee, chaired by old Etonian Sir Benny Cusack-Smith, a local JP. His ranks were swelled by the absorption of the Brighton OMS and the support of the Rotary Club. The Town Council itself produced some helpers, with Councillor Davis putting in sterling service before moving on to become the County Commander for the British Fascists Sussex Area 97 in 1927.

The Chief Constable of Brighton, Charles Griffin, had previous experience of putting down civil unrest. His police duties had precluded his serving in the trenches, but he saw action in Luton in 1919, when his brutal suppression of an ex-servicemen's demonstration led to a riot that saw the Town Hall burnt to the ground.

He knew the importance of mounted special constables and set about recruiting three squadrons, each under the command of serving or retired colonels. Unfortunately suitable volunteers were not forthcoming in the town itself so Harry Preston, hotel owner and boxing promoter, went into the rural hinterland in search of troopers. In a short time a mixture including yeoman farmers and retired officers had been found to make up the numbers.

The General Strike started on 4 May, and in Brighton 6,000 men in the transport and printing trades stopped work. On that first morning there were no trams, buses, trains or newspapers. A week later the strike in Brighton was growing, as more workers from other trades joined in. Relations with the regular police had been largely cordial, but there had been several attempts by the specials to provoke a response from the strikers, particularly at mass meetings. These had been unsuccessful, until the 11 May.

Rumours had gone round the town that there would be an attempt that day to get trams out of the depot on Lewes Road (on the site of the present-day bus garage). By midday a crowd of 1,500 interested but mostly uninvolved bystanders had gathered, a figure that was swollen to more than 3,000 by large numbers of mothers who were collecting their children for lunch. The manager of the depot had come out and asked the crowd to disperse, with the warning that 200 police were on their way, but to no effect. At around 12.30 p.m. the infantry specials arrived, followed by the Chief Constable in a car. He got out, and according to one eyewitness, with no warning issued, he blew his whistle.

This was the signal for the horses to come forward, and they started to move into the people on the pavement,

The 'specials' cavalry charge – they became known as the 'Black and Tans'. (Vanessa Woodward: reproduced with the kind permission of Andy Durr)

pushing them against the wall. Fear was growing in the crowd, as women and children were being crushed, and then the mounted specials charged into the crowd with batons drawn, striking out at whoever was in their path.

One man, who was protecting a panic-stricken 10-year-old girl, turned to the specials and said, 'I appeal to you as Englishmen.' He managed to push the girl to safety as a special reared up in front of him, whilst a regular batoned him across his shoulder.

Many of the women and children had now fled into Saunders Park, but there was no respite as the horsemen steeplechased over the wall in pursuit. A 70-year-old man had turned to a young policeman in the park and told him he was old enough to be his grandfather – the special proceeded to back his horse into him, causing him to fall over, and then hit him with his long truncheon.

Near the gates to the park stood Harry Preston's friend, music hall star George Robey, armed with a knuckle-duster and proclaiming loudly that what the police really needed was a few tanks. Despite such provocation he was ignored by the crowd.

In response to the attacks most tried to flee as best they could, but a few fought back and attempted to protect their retreat, and twenty-two men were arrested. In the ensuing melee two civilians were seriously wounded, and many others sustained lesser injuries. Subsequent press coverage made no mention of these casualties, although the damaged eye sustained by one of the police officers was widely reported.

'I sentence you to 6 months' hard labour.'
(Vanessa Woodward: reproduced with the kind permission of Andy Durr)

Some hours later the twenty-two manacled men were marched back to the Town Hall in the centre of a phalanx of mounted and foot police officers. The following day they appeared before the Magistrates Bench, chaired by the Mayor. They were represented by the Labour Councillor for Lewes Road, but he was not allowed to speak to them before the trial, and his request for time to do so was turned down flat.

For the next six hours the defendants, none of whom had a previous conviction, were charged with incitement to riot and assaulting police officers. At the end of the session they were all found guilty and received prison sentences ranging from one to six months of hard labour. In his summing up the Mayor opined that 'the police exercised great care in the execution of their duties and did not act in anything that might be described as an officious manner'.

Whilst the court had been in session the TUC had called off the strike, which was added cause for rejoicing in the ensuing civic celebrations held to thank the police, and particularly the specials, for their role in preventing a purported revolution. At one such dinner the Mayor thanked the specials for 'having shewn the hooligans and rough element that mob law would not be allowed to reign in Brighton'. Demonstrating a sense of balance intrinsic to his civic position, he went on to assert that he was not against trade unionism in its proper place, although 'it would have been better if the agitators had been sent to prison rather than the misguided people' he had sent down the previous week.

As the specials were stood down and departed from Brighton to go back to their homes, for many of the strikers there would be no similar return to work. The employers took their revenge by taking the opportunity to rewrite terms of employment for those they took back, whilst blacklisting those they thought to be heavily involved in the organisation of the strike. For those considered to be ringleaders it was either hard labour or no labour.

AD 1928–1935

THE FIGHT FOR
THE SOUTH DOWNS

ONE OF THE longest and most keenly contested battles of the inter-war period was fought over the plans by Brighton Corporation (as the council was then known) to give approval for the construction of a motor-racing circuit of some 5 miles in size, by a private business consortium on land that it owned on the Downs near Devil's Dyke. The opposition to this planned track was led by the East Sussex County Council based at Lewes, supported by the local landowners and the embryonic environmental movement, particularly The Society of Sussex Downsmen.

This was not the first time that the urban interests of Brighton had clashed with those of its rural hinterland in East Sussex. Brighton, keen to protect its reputation as a healthy resort, had sought on a number of occasions to impose conditions on farmers and the produce that they sold into the town, with good reason. Between 1896 and 1900 a total of fifty-five cattle had been found to be infected with TB on entering its slaughterhouses, and in 1900 an outbreak of twenty-five cases of scarlet fever was traced to a dairy farm outside the town's borders.

On the surrounding downs the growth of smallholdings led to a serious problem with unsealed cesspits, cesspools and pigsties leaking their putrid contents into the permeable chalk layers that supplied the town with its water. In all of these episodes the County Council at Lewes tried to water down the legislation and protect the financial interests of their farmers.

Brighton had started to purchase the surrounding countryside to protect its water supply, and by the end of the 1920s the Corporation owned much of the land beyond even the recently extended borders. Well in advance of the Green Belt Act of 1938 the town had already secured a large swathe of downland, and secured it from unco-ordinated development. By the end of the Second World War virtually all of the adjoining rural area was under Brighton's ownership.

It was on one such piece of land, which actually lay within the newly enlarged Portslade Council's

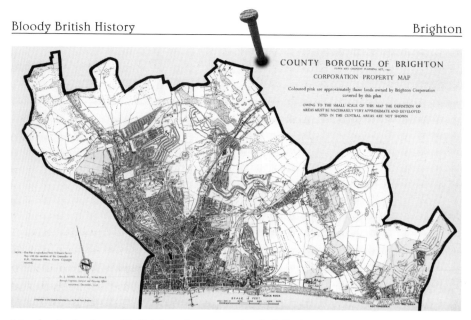

Map showing land owned by Brighton Corporation (unshaded). (DJB)

boundaries, that the proposed development would take place, on a tract of land known more in accuracy than romance as Adders' Bottom. With the advent of the scheme there was also an apparent role reversal, as East Sussex County Council, seemingly forgetting its previous record of promoting pollution and pestilence, now proclaimed itself to be the saviour of the unspoilt natural beauty of the Downs.

In this it was supported by a majority of the few large-scale landlords who owned most of the Downs between Brighton and Lewes. Their backing might be seen as a little hypocritical as they had been selling off plots of land for house building, whilst elsewhere quarrying out large chunks of chalk to provide cement for the development boom of the inter-war period.

The racetrack saga started with an initial proposal in 1926, and continued on and off for another ten years until 1935. At first the County Council's response was fairly muted. The best that it could come up with was a minor intervention from the Agricultural Committee under that much feared piece of legislation, The Injurious Weeds Order. Brighton was told off about the state of the track site, which was allegedly 'derelict and very full of weeds, especially docks', and was ordered to destroy them before they could seed.

There was also some discussion about enforcing the petrol filling station by-laws, the planned racetrack being in an area where petrol stations were prohibited, a consideration of perhaps greater importance than the rampant weed growth, given the proposed use of the site.

A number of letters protesting against the track were sent to Brighton Corporation, including one from the Sisters of St Mary's Convent, 'a refuge for destitute girls', which feared that 'the work of the convent would be rendered virtually impossible' by the proximity of the racetrack. It seems more likely that a greater threat to 'the work of the convent' may have been posed by the boys at the neighbouring Mile Oak Approved School.

Despite the initial weakness of the opposition to the racetrack, the promoter of the scheme, Lawrence Clayton, secretary of the Brighton and Hove Motor Club, was unable to raise funds in the midst of the 1920s recession. By the time he came back with his final proposal in 1933 the order of battle had changed.

Ranged against Brighton Corporation was a large coalition of interests co-ordinated from the County Council offices in Lewes, including a wide range of local councils, heritage organisations and of course the landowners. Their plan was to get Parliament to pass a piece of legislation known as the South Downs Protection Bill, which would preclude any development on the Downs.

This grand coalition suffered an early setback in the elections for Portslade Council in 1934. These were important as the track was located within Portslade's boundaries and needed that council's permission to proceed. Clayton had organised several well attended and lively meetings to discuss the plans, at which it became clear that the existing councillors were not representative of the largely working-class population of that urban district, who were keen for any project that increased employment opportunities.

'What do you mean, there's no petrol?' (Giorgiomontefiori)

There were five seats up for grabs at the polls, and four candidates stood on the single issue of supporting the development of the race circuit. They trounced the opposition, and in the absence of a fifth pro-track candidate, the final seat went to an independent ratepayer.

Over in Lewes the unfortunate clerk to the County Council, Hugh McIlveen, was up against it from the start. After the disaster at Portslade an official was sent to investigate and received a hostile reception from the locals, most of whom refused to talk to him. McIlveen was also having more predictable difficulties with Brighton, whose help he needed in putting his bill together.

This was particularly so in respect of maps and surveys, which at the less well-funded Lewes administration were in short supply. An increasingly desperate McIlveen wrote in the polite official fashion of the time to his opposite number at Brighton: 'I am sorry that you could not see your way to fall in with the suggestion that the County Surveyor should see your Surveyor.' What he actually meant was: 'I am really very angry that you are being so obstructive.'

In response, J.G. Drew, the Brighton Assistant Town Clerk, wrote back to tell him that, 'I am not disposed to give your surveyor a roving commission'. This was the polite way of telling him he could shove it. The maps that eventually accompanied the bill were dated 1894!

As the bill was heard before a committee of Parliament the coalition started to fall apart. Exemptions for housing estates and/or quarrying had to be granted to all of the private landlords, including the Lords Gage and Buxton who had been so vociferous in their defence of the Downs from development (on land other than that which they owned).

The *Brighton Herald* had described the bill's purpose as being 'designed to hand over control of the Downs to some committee of autocratic County gentlemen', and the self-serving actions of the landlords did little to assuage this portrayal.

The local councils also ran for cover when they realised how much the bill could end up costing them, including Hove who were the largest contributor to the East Sussex County budget. In the end the South Downs Preservation Bill fell by the wayside, where it met the failed racetrack plans of Lawrence Clayton, who had yet again been unable to convince investors as to the worth of his scheme.

AD 1934

TRUNK MURDERS PART 2

A LITTLE OVER 100 years after John Holloway had been executed for the murder of his wife Celia, Brighton was to be haunted by not just one but two similar cases in the summer of 1934, involving dead women being stored in trunks. Despite the considerable efforts of the police, both cases would remain unresolved.

TRUNK CASE NO. 1

On 17 June a porter at Brighton Station discovered an unpleasant smell emanating from a trunk that had been deposited in the unclaimed-luggage office on Derby Day, several weeks before. The police were called and upon opening it discovered the torso of a woman. The following day her legs were found wrapped in a parcel at Kings Cross Station. The pathologist described her as being in her twenties, with well-manicured toenails, and said that she would have been healthy when she was alive. She was also five months pregnant.

Her identity remained a mystery, as well as the cause of her death. Her pregnancy suggested to Chief Inspector Donaldson of Scotland Yard that her death may have been the result of an attempted abortion, and he had Dr Edward Massiah put under surveillance. Massiah was known to have a fairly exclusive list of patients, and it has been suggested that Donaldson was quietly advised to focus his investigation elsewhere. Despite following up on over 500 separate leads the police remained unable to identify the victim, and the case remains unsolved to this day.

TRUNK CASE NO. 2

In the course of their enquiries the police had been tracking down women who had suddenly disappeared over the past few months, and one name that had come up was that of Violette Kaye, who had not been seen since early May. Her partner, Toni Mancini, was interviewed on 14 July, and detectives, suspicious as to his story, searched his flat in

Violette Kaye. (Rodhullandemu)

Kemp Street the following day. Mancini had fled to London that morning, leaving behind a trunk in which the body of Violette was found. He was arrested two days later on the road to Sidcup, and charged with murder.

Mancini and Kaye had met in London, and moved to Brighton the year before. Kaye's occupation was designated as that of a 'professional dancer', the contemporary term used for describing a prostitute. Mancini, a small-time crook, had lived off her earnings since they had been in town. They had recently taken lodgings in Park Crescent, where a regular visitor had been a mature bookmaker, Charles Moores, who they both referred to as 'Uncle'. 'Sugar Daddy' might have been a more appropriate familial reference, as he gave Kaye money, a radio set and had organised the conversion of the flat to electric lighting.

Moores had been driven to Park Crescent on each occasion by his driver, a man by the name of Kerslake who lived in Franklin Road. On his last visit on 4 May, Moores told Kaye that he was being admitted to a psychiatric institution that night, and wouldn't be around for a while. The very next day Mancini took a job at the Skylark Café on the seafront, his first employment in over a year. The sugar had stopped flowing.

The following week Violette had turned up at the Skylark a little worse for the wear, and there was a minor scene as she berated Mancini for flirting with a waitress. She left at around 3.30 p.m., and was apparently last seen alive a few hours later at Park Crescent, by the driver Kerslake. He claimed that she appeared to be anxious and under the influence of drugs. The reason for his visit, Moores now being in an institution, was never questioned, but his evidence – that he heard men inside the flat, and saw another arriving as he left – was taken as gospel. Mancini claimed that when he arrived home at 7.30 p.m. he found Violette dead on their bed.

Fearful as to how this would look to the police, given his criminal record, Mancini claimed he hid the body, first in a cupboard, and then in a trunk. In an echo of Holloway's grisly journey a century before, Mancini took the trunk on a handcart to his new lodgings at Kemp Street. Indeed, at some point on London Road he would have crossed paths with the route Holloway took.

The case was initially heard at Brighton magistrates' court in August, before being transferred to the assizes at Lewes in December. Norman Birkett, KC, led the defence at Lewes, and his advocacy on behalf of Mancini has been widely, if not enthusiastically, acclaimed. It should be noted that his case was largely based on that presented previously by F.H. Carpenter at the magistrates' court, to whom some of the perhaps dubious credit should be given.

The police investigation had thrown up many witnesses who had heard Mancini make incriminating statements, in clubs, cafés, and not just around the town of Brighton but in London as well. There was also a range of physical evidence including a burnt hammer head found at Park Crescent, possibly the murder weapon. Then there was the telegram he had sent to Violette's sister on 11 May, cancelling her planned visit the following week, and purporting to be from Violette herself, as she was going to France.

In court Birkett made persistent attacks on the prosecution case, the character of the witnesses and that of the victim herself. Kaye's occupation and her consumption of alcohol and morphine were repeatedly brought forward, and it was suggested that her death might have been the result of her having fallen down the stairs in a drugged stupor.

A number of the witnesses were also 'professional dancers', including Joan Tinn, a 'dancing instructress' who was living in a tent in a field in Rottingdean, known as Klondyke Field. Birkett suggested that her statement, in which she claimed Mancini had told her that he would make Brighton famous, had been coerced by the police.

The waters were further muddied by the allegation that Violette's ex-lover, Kay Fredericks, then working at the headquarters of the British Union of Fascists, had been jealous of Mancini. By now fascism was becoming something of a dirty word following Hitler's accession to power in Germany and street violence in Britain. Indeed, fascist leader Oswald Moseley and three of his BUF colleagues were currently on trial in another court at Lewes, for inciting a riot in Worthing some months previously.

The defence plan had been to throw as much mud as possible at the prosecution case in the hope that some of it would stick. It did. The jury, all male, took just over two hours to find Mancini not guilty. He was stunned, and spent some time with his head in his hands, before leaving the court a free man.

The flat in Kemp Street, with the trunk on the left. (Rodhullandemu)

While Toni Mancini was baring his soul to the British press in 1976, another similarly grisly story was unfolding on the other side of the world in Singapore. A British businessman, Michael Culley, had murdered his wife shortly after arriving in the Far East. He had dismembered her body and stored it in a trunk in his flat. He then told his 14-year-old son of the murder.

On the death of his father two years later, Culley junior, now sixteen and living in England, told the police about his father's crime and the body was recovered. In his statement he said that he had not reported it earlier as he loved his father.

Had Mancini really murdered Violette, unhappy at the prospect of having to now earn a living? Or alternatively, had he murdered Violette, jealous that she would now have to go back to earning a living? Had the driver Kerslake connived with Mancini to provide an element of doubt, through the claim of having seen other men at Park Crescent that afternoon? Might Kerslake himself have been the murderer? The answer to these questions will probably never be known. In further echoes of John Holloway, Mancini would in 1976 confess to the crime, in a *News of the World* interview for which he was no doubt financially rewarded. Some ten years later, speaking to a reporter from the local paper, he changed his story again, denying any involvement in either case. The only certainty for the two unfortunate women was that no one would ever be brought to justice for their killings.

Toni Mancini. (Rodhullandemu)

AD 1940

INVASION ALERT!

BY **THE SUMMER** of 1940, Hitler's triumphant armies had conquered Poland, Norway, France and the Low Countries. They had reached the Channel ports and their focus fell upon their next target, Britain. Whilst the British had managed to save much of the Royal Air Force, and of course had the Royal Navy to guard the sea approaches, on the ground the army was less well prepared for the defence of the realm.

Despite the miracle of Dunkirk, and the equally remarkable evacuation of a further 200,000 troops from north-western France, the British Army was in poor shape. In July there were only twenty-eight under-strength and under-equipped divisions to be spread from Scotland to Land's End. This weakness in numbers and quality was further compounded by the poor allocation of the divisions.

Churchill and the Chiefs of Staff, expecting the invasion to come on the east coast, had positioned the bulk of their forces to meet this scenario, leaving just five divisions, with three in reserve, to cover the south coast between Dover and Land's End. Churchill was dubious as to the chances of success for a German invasion. He thought it would be very difficult for them to land on the east coast, and further added that, 'Even more unlikely is it that the south coast would be attacked.' In the middle of August the Chiefs of Staff confirmed this outlook: 'We seem at present to be slightly over-insured along the south coast.'

At around the same time at German Headquarters the invasion plan, codenamed Operation Sea Lion, was being finessed. The original plan had called for landings between Dover and Lyme Regis in Dorset, but following naval concerns over supplying the bridgeheads, this was narrowed to the area between Brighton in the west and Folkestone in the east.

The plan proposed to land nine divisions in the first assault wave, three of which, from the 9th Army, were to land between Beachy Head and Brighton. Specialist mountain troops had been drafted in to climb the chalk cliffs where necessary. The Brighton area

German aerial reconnaissance photo of Brighton. (Reproduced with the kind permission of the Royal Pavilion and Museums: Brighton and Hove)

was to be further targeted by an airborne division being dropped onto the Downs behind the town, in order to prevent reinforcements arriving and to cut off the escape route of those already there. Arriving with the second wave would be the 1st SS Panzer Division Liebstandarte, Hitler's personal bodyguard and responsible for the massacre a few months before of eighty POWs from the Royal Warwickshire Regiment.

In early September the British had noticed that invasion barges were being concentrated in the French Channel ports, and finally the penny dropped as to where the invasion would come. As a result of this a further eight divisions were brought down to the south coast by the middle of that month. On 17 September, Hitler, concerned about the inability of Goering's Luftwaffe to control the skies above the landing grounds, cancelled the invasion.

The British of course did not know of this, and invasion precautions would remain in place for much of the war,

being replaced eventually by similar measures to ensure the secrecy of the Allies' own plans, which culminated in the D-Day landings nearly four years later. The people of Brighton would have to become used to the restrictions of daily life in a 'Defence Area'.

They were also acutely conscious of the possibility of the enemy arriving from the sky, some having already come fluttering down in their parachutes during the Battle of Britain. It seems a rather firm approach had been adopted by civilians when apprehending downed foreign airmen, regardless of whose side they were fighting on. This led to an official notice being published in the *Brighton Herald* stating that whilst continued vigilance was required, 'it is emphasised that only in the event of parachutists adopting a threatening attitude or attempting to commit hostile acts should force be used.' It went on to explain that the parachutist might be one of our European Allies, and 'therefore the public are asked to exercise great care and discretion.'

Restrictions on visitors and curfews were a particular problem for many businesses in the Defence Area resort towns along the coast. At what should have been the height of the season in August 1940, the Sussex Mayor's Association met in Brighton to consider a resolution to examine 'specific proposals for averting extreme financial disaster in the Defence Area.' The Mayor of Hastings introduced the motion, stating that the removal of schools and the departure of wealthy residents, on top of the ban on visitors, had placed an intolerable burden on the local economy. Such were the concerns of the chambers of commerce, blissfully ignorant of the possibility of imminent inward German divestment.

With the exception of the seafront, the curfew would be relaxed during the winter months when invasion was thought to be impossible, much to the relief of the large number of commuters who were still travelling to and from London for work. There were many occasions when late working or delayed trains had meant they had arrived at Brighton Station after curfew, and had to camp there for the night before jumping straight back on the train in the morning. On the bright side, it would appear that leaves on the line or the wrong kind of snow were not the perils that they seem to be for the present-day rail traveller.

In 1944, with preparations for D-Day underway, Brighton and its surrounds became a Protected Area. The first prosecutions for entering the protected area 'without the permission of the Secretary of State for War' were brought before the courts that May. The two women concerned had come down to spend the weekend in Brighton at the invitation of two Canadian officers they knew. All four were in a taxi when a policeman stopped it as it was leaving the station, and were promptly put on the next train back. Despite such bona-fides the women were fined £2 each. The cases were heard in their absence as they were carrying out important war work.

With the successful invasion of France restrictions were relaxed and promenades reopened, but the beach remained out of bounds as defences were removed and the work of mine clearance began. Rumours that it would be fifteen years before the beach was safe began to circulate, and the *Brighton Herald* suggested that a new 'secret

The beach was off limits. (Reproduced with the kind permission of the Royal Pavilion and Museums: Brighton and Hove)

weapon', the 'water gun', might be used. Whatever the merits of this glorified hose-pipe, the donkey work of mine clearance fell to the men of the bomb disposal units.

The mines intended for Hitler's invaders had already claimed the life of a Canadian soldier taking a shortcut across the Downs, whilst on exercise in 1944. They would claim another life shortly after the war in Europe had finished, when a mine that Captain Revis was removing from the West Pier exploded. He had been a popular and respected man in the town, having successfully rendered safe over 200 unexploded bombs during the war, including one in Patcham that weighed 1,000 pounds. He was one of over sixty men who died clearing 100,000 mines from the beaches between the Wash and Chichester, in the final year of the war and the period just after.

Despite the best efforts of the land-based disposal teams, the storms that hit Brighton that year were just a little more dangerous than usual, as the flotsam and jetsam of war continued to wash up on the shore. Two large mines appeared on the beach that September, and a dozen more were washed up in October. They have long since ceased to be a threat, and if there were any left they would have long ago been discovered by the massed ranks of metal detectorists who appear at dawn on a summer morning.

DRUNK ON DUTY

The Home Guard started life as the Local Defence Volunteers in the desperate days of May 1940. Within twenty-four hours of the call to muster, the Worthing Battalion of the Sussex Home Guard was the first on patrol. Despite such a rapid response, it was not without its problems, as one MP noted in the House of Commons: 'In one company in East Sussex there are six different generals all dressed up as generals.'

Eventually things settled down into a routine, although there was one night in 1943 when the High Command perhaps had reason to be grateful that Hitler was otherwise involved in Russia. A Canadian had been given the key to the flat of a woman who managed a soldiers' club in town, so that he could stay there for the night. In his drunken state he stopped and asked a local Home Guard unit for directions, and ever eager to serve they escorted him there.

Wishing to show his gratitude the regular offered them the hospitality of the premises, and considering it rude to refuse, the three young men consumed six bottles of champagne, before returning to their guard room with another half dozen bottles. Two of them were found comatose several hours later in the restroom, surrounded by half empty champagne bottles, whilst the third was eventually revived, after fifteen minutes under the cold tap, to the point where he could remember what had happened.

In court the magistrates found that the Canadian had been too drunk to be capable of forming an intention to steal, and thus the charges against him were dismissed. The Home Guards were punished with stinking hangovers and extra duties.

AD 1940–1944

THE BRIGHTON BLITZ

BRIGHTON WAS FORTUNATE in the early years of the war to escape the mass air raids that caused so much devastation to places like London, Coventry and Portsmouth. The occasional bombs that were dropped on the town during this period had mostly been intended for other destinations and usually caused little real damage.

However, Brighton's luck ran out on 14 September 1940, when a single German plane, presumably separated from the rest of its squadron, caused the heaviest casualties the town would suffer in the whole war. As the bomber traversed the town from east to west it dropped its payload from Kemptown to Hove, killing fifty-five people in the process and wounding many more. Tragedy, shock and stoicism followed in its wake.

The duty manager at the Kemptown Odeon had announced from the stage that there was an air-raid warning, but perhaps lulled into a false sense of security by the lack of previous bombing, everyone kept their seats. The manager had just got to the front lobby when the cinema took a direct hit. The film they had been watching was *It Could Happen to You*.

One mother was beside herself with worry – she had sent her two sons to the Odeon for the afternoon and they had not returned home. She had looked for them amongst the unfortunate children who had died, but to no avail. A few hours later they walked through the front door unblemished. When asked where they had been, they replied: 'We went to the Odeon but it had just been bombed, so we went to a different cinema down the road.' Another bomb had landed nearby

The Kemptown Odeon took a direct hit. (Reproduced with the kind permission of the Royal Pavilion and Museums: Brighton and Hove)

An ARP Warden seeking divine help in the argument with the regional commissioners? (Reproduced with the kind permission of the Royal Pavilion and Museums: Brighton and Hove)

in Upper Bedford Street, demolishing houses and shops on both sides of the road, and taking more lives.

Meanwhile, at Hove cricket ground, a large crowd had gathered for what would perhaps be the last chance to see a strong Sussex team. They had started well, hitting more than 150 runs in a match to raise money for the Brighton and Hove Spitfire Fund. As the sound of the bombing in East Brighton reached the crease and the local air-raid warning sounded, the players had initially decided to stay at the wicket.

Suddenly someone shouted 'Look out!' and the players hit the deck as the heavy thud of a delayed-action bomb landing nearby was followed by a shower of displaced earth. As some of

the crowd took cover, others proceeded in an orderly fashion to the exits, just as another bomb dug a hole in one corner of the ground. The situation was now getting pretty serious so, after a hurried consultation between the umpires and the captains, it was decided that this would be a good time to take the tea interval. Unfortunately for those still waiting patiently for the players to come back out, the police intervened and ordered the evacuation of the ground. It became known at the cricket ground as the day 'Hitler stopped play'.

Despite its gentle introduction to aerial warfare, Brighton had prepared well in advance for the potential perils it could bring. The ARP service had been activated early in 1939, with a core of paid wardens supported by a larger number of unpaid volunteers. The paid wardens had numbered 396 at the start of the war, but had been successively cut to 300 and then to 250, along with the budget provided by the government.

Matters came to a head in late 1940 when the Regional Commissioners decreed that a further ninety-eight men were to be dismissed. Whilst this may have reflected the need to divert resources to those cities suffering the full force of the Blitz, it did not go down well in Brighton, which was itself now experiencing more frequent attacks. A meeting of delegates representing the 1,250 volunteers agreed to set up what was effectively a trade union, the Warden's Association. Its first action was to refuse to carry out certain routine maintenance tasks, although emergencies were to remain unaffected.

The dedication of the ARPs would be further tested a few months later in April 1941, this time by the actions of their local superiors on the Emergency Committee for Brighton. The wardens were sifting through a bombed row of houses for survivors, but were instructed to stand down between 7 p.m. and 7 a.m., due to the dangerous condition of some neighbouring walls. The ARPs felt they should carry on regardless and two of them talked of resigning in protest. The Committee caused uproar when it suspended the two men, and after two nights of enforced idleness the curfew was removed and the men reinstated. The following day a mother and two of her children were rescued alive after being trapped in the rubble for fifty-two hours.

As the Blitz subsided elsewhere, Brighton now became the focus of hit-and-run raids by small groups of

ROCKET ATTACK

Just as the people of Sussex thought they could relax from the fear of aerial attacks, they were to discover that there was one last sting in the tail of Hitler's war machine.

In the latter part of 1944 there was a new sound in the skies above: that of the recently developed V1 flying bomb. People soon learned that as long as it could be heard they were relatively safe. It was when the motor stopped that it went into its descent, to come crashing down bringing death and devastation with it. Most were targeted for the London area, but 886 landed in Sussex.

As the V1 launch sites on the Continent were overrun by the advancing Allies, the danger receded, to be replaced by that of the longer range and more powerful V2 rockets. These made no announcement of their arrival and would appear literally out of the blue. Fortunately only four V2s came to earth in the county. Finally the citizens of Brighton could get on with life, with the only danger from above coming out of the back end of a seagull.

planes from across the Channel. These went on with some regularity for the next three years and typically involved the indiscriminate machine-gunning of anything that came into the path of the raiders, accompanied by the release of a variety of bombs. The largest such raid occurred on 24 May 1943, when twenty-four planes attacked the town, killing twenty-four people in the process.

Around this time an old man astonished his rescuers, who had been labouring all day to free him from his ruined home. As he accepted their help to escape from his refuge, he said, 'Well, I'm off to get a livener folks!', and disappeared in the direction of the nearest undamaged pub. On another occasion a husband and wife were watching from their bedroom window as two low-flying planes came towards them. 'Look at the Spitfires,' said the wife. 'They're not Spitfires, they're Messerschmitts!' shouted the husband above the sound of incoming bullets as they dived to the floor in a shower of broken glass.

As late as July 1943 children were still being evacuated from Brighton as the hit-and-run missions continued. The last major casualties were sustained in February 1944, when another ten people died in one attack. The final raid was just before D-Day, on 3 June 1944. During the war the town had more than 1,700 alerts and fifty-six actual raids. One hundred and ninety-eight of its citizens were killed and 357 suffered serious injuries. More than 200 houses

Air-raid shelter with bathroom at the far end – hope no one's desperate, as there's no loo roll. (Reproduced with the kind permission of the Royal Pavilion and Museums: Brighton and Hove)

were destroyed and 894 were seriously damaged, many of them in the poorer parts of town. Fourteen thousand were slightly damaged.

Whilst the death toll was mercifully low compared to other towns and cities, these figures demonstrate that the people of Brighton were on the front line of the aerial war for far longer. With an average of just over one alert a day for the full four-year period, the shelters really would have been a home from home. Furthermore the nature of the low-level attacks and the ubiquitous strafing with machine guns and cannons must have made them feel much more personal and immediate.

AD 1940–1945

WARTIME CRIME

CAREFUL SCRUTINY OF the *Brighton Herald* suggests that there were three distinct groups who kept the forces of law and order busy during the war: juveniles, Canadians and Americans.

The Chief Constable in his review of 1940 was pleased to announce a drop in overall crime levels, but expressed his concern at the 'black spot on the social life of the community' represented by juvenile offences. The number of offences had risen from 244 in 1939, to a total of 412 the following year, a third of all indictable offences. The Education Committee was similarly concerned at levels of underage drinking, particularly the sight of young girls in pubs drinking beer with whisky chasers.

As if to rubber-stamp such assertions, a meeting of the Brighton Cinemas Association complained of gangs of youths who were vandalising their cinemas, ripping out light fittings, seats and bathroom fixtures. One cinema manager complained that, so frequent were his requests for replacements, his head office had enquired as to whether he was trying to do a complete refurbishment on the quiet.

By 1942 the Chief Constable was able to report that the situation had been brought under control by placing the ringleaders in approved schools. The success of this approach was brought into question several weeks later when two graduates of these institutions were re-arrested, escaped remand and re-offended again in a two-boy crime wave in the London Road area. One of the fifteen year olds had already been birched once and sent to approved school twice in relation to previous offences.

Evacuees arrived at Brighton Station whilst the Chief Constable worried about juvenile crime. (Reproduced with the kind permission of the Royal Pavilion and Museums: Brighton and Hove)

There were of course a number of arrests for the usual shoplifting, looting and theft cases, and possibly a little ahead of his time, there was the doctor who made over two dozen prescriptions for 100 grams of cocaine. Most of this he claimed was for an 'anti-Hitler tonic' he made, the strength of which varied according to the 'nerve tension of the war'.

The arrival of 200,000 Canadians, many of them in Sussex, provided a new challenge for the constabulary. Their arrival to bolster Britain's weak defences in her hour of need was greatly appreciated. The accompanying wave of promiscuity, drinking and fighting was less welcome in certain quarters.

Frustrated by their inactivity, some soldiers let off steam on the streets of Brighton. In one incident near the Clocktower, three Canadians were eventually arrested by the police following a fierce struggle. In their defence their officer reflected on some of these tensions as he told the court: 'They are good soldiers and when they had an opportunity of proving it they did very well.'

A few months later one of their number smashed twenty-three shop windows as he drunkenly traversed Western Road. He vigorously resisted arrest, and one of the police officers who had been present told the court: 'I struck him with my truncheon, but it did not seem to take effect.' In his defence the Canadian stated that, 'the last thing I remember I was at the Regent Dance Hall. I had been drinking and the next morning I woke up in a cell.'

'Where's the girls?' Canadian soldiers at the Pavilion. (Reproduced with the kind permission of the Royal Pavilion and Museums: Brighton and Hove)

The author Terence Robertson has suggested that many Sussex matrons 'were quickly convinced that Canadians generally were the most dangerous threat to youthful virginity ever encountered.' In the absence of a large proportion of the local men, the Canadians were generally welcomed by the women of Sussex. Both perspectives are supported by the fact that when the soldiers returned home, over 40,000 British wives and 20,000 children were accompanying them.

There were, however, a few relationships that had less happy endings. Jealousy got the better of several of the young men when their girlfriends moved on. This was not a good thing with so many guns around in the build-up to D-Day. One despatch rider shot his ex with a revolver, after she went into an American bar on West Street to meet a friend. Another set up a Bren gun in a garden opposite his former lover's house in Mile Oak Road, killing her and wounding her new man. The hangman's noose awaited these men, and several others who had committed similar crimes.

These were also the days of unsafe back-street abortions, and several women died as a result of the dangers attached to such procedures being carried out by untrained practitioners without medical facilities. One newly arrived soldier had set up shop in Tichborne Street, but was charged with manslaughter after his fifth client died. The wife of a Canadian officer, who was away on service, met a similar end after visiting a local woman for her help.

After several years of waiting the Canadians finally got to do what they had come over for, and set off for Normandy. Some had already been across to Dieppe on a disastrous raid in 1942, including one soldier whose court case for assaulting a policeman had to be adjourned, as he was fighting his way back off the beach at the due time for his appearance in front of the magistrates. Most of the townsfolk of Brighton would miss the Canadians, who had always been keen to help where they could, particularly after air raids. No doubt the police also wished them well, glad that they were now fighting the Nazis, and not themselves.

The Americans (or 'overseas soldiers' as the *Herald* referred to them) arrived on the scene later, but rapidly made their contribution to the crime statistics. A captain attacked a husband and wife in a seafront hotel and several other civilians were beaten up in separate incidents, but it was to be in armed robbery that they really excelled.

A café on Marlborough Place was held up by three 'overseas soldiers', but a more impressive haul was made by the robbers of the post office in College Street, Kemptown, who arrived bearing a machine gun. The escalation in the fire arms used as the war progressed is neatly illustrated by a post office robbery in Woodingdean during 1940, some four years previously. On that occasion the British robber had come equipped with only a shotgun, purchased the same day with a cheque that bounced.

Not all such attempts were so successful, as one American found to his cost when he threatened a passing petty officer with what he said was a concealed gun. The sailor put him down

'Where's the Canadians?' Land Army girls taking a break. (Reproduced with the kind permission of the Royal Pavilion and Museums: Brighton and Hove)

AFTERS …

The restriction on permitted hours of opening for pubs, brought in during the First World War, was seen by many in the drinking classes as something of a disaster. Yet for every dark cloud there was a silver lining. Without the constraints of the new closing times, introduced under the Defence of the Realm Act, there would never have been that fine British social tradition of after-hours drinking.

The youth of today may enjoy the opportunity to get hammered at all hours of the day, but they will never know the feeling of pride and acceptance that could be generated that first time you were invited to 'stop on'. No longer were you cast out onto the streets by the landlord at 11 p.m. You were now a part of that pre-closing ritual, nursing a pint in a secluded and privileged corner as the rest of the pub was cleared out. The last customer gone, mein host would draw the curtains and for the next few hours, or longer if need be, the world was put to rights as the beer kept flowing.

The good people of Brighton were not going to allow the arrival of another world war, and the best efforts of Adolf Hitler and the local constabulary, to upset this by now well entrenched tradition. A number of premises received mentions in (the *Brighton Herald*) despatches for service in this respect:

- **The Spitfire Club:** This hostelry had been set up in premises that had previously been the Marlborough House School, and was raided early one morning in 1941. To gain entrance the front door bell had to rung three times, then again at the side door. This granted access to a kitchen, where a cupboard hid a small hole that had been cut in the wall, leading into the bar area. Around twenty punters were discovered, half of whom were serving RAF and army officers. In their defence the RAF officers, all pilots from a fighter squadron, claimed that they were on leave and needed to relax.

- **The Mitre Tavern:** In early 1942 this pub was under surveillance by several policemen, who had reason to believe that illicit drinking was going on. One officer reported that he had heard 'the chink of glasses and ringing of the till in the bar', whilst another heard various voices saying 'a drop of rum', 'gin and lime' and '3s 10d'. All were found guilty of being on the premises for 'a purpose other than one of immediate and urgent necessity'. The defendants may have felt this was a somewhat subjective judgement on the part of the magistrates.

- **The Compton Arms:** The landlord had been 'entertaining friends at his own expense' one morning when the law knocked on his door. This perfectly legitimate activity was also frequently used as an excuse to cover an 'afters' session, and this was no doubt on the minds of the magistrates who found them guilty. He successfully appealed this verdict: perhaps the appellant court were more sympathetic to, and indeed enjoyers of, this now gone but not forgotten British tradition.

with one punch and followed through with several more, before discovering the only thing in the would-be robber's pocket was his hand.

At the end of the war Brighton played host to large numbers of recently liberated South African and Australian prisoners of war, on their way back home from Europe. Their stay was brief and without criminal incident. Having just escaped from imprisonment, they were presumably in no mood to be locked up again.

AD 1964–1981

MODS AND ROCKERS

BRIGHTON HAD BEEN no stranger to mob violence, but the Bank Holiday disorders associated with the Mods and Rockers in the sixties were of a different order of magnitude, in size if not in casualties.

The first major confrontations had taken place at Clacton and Margate on Easter weekend in 1964. Large groups of young men and women had been running up and down the promenade, causing some damage and getting into a few fights. Even when they went to sleep they upset the local equilibrium by slumbering wherever they could, on the beach and on grass verges. Even those who booked in at local caravan parks came in for criticism, one magistrate describing such unsupervised sites as being 'conducive to non-moral types'.

Over 100 arrests were made at Clacton, including one young man who was charged with 'loitering with intent to steal'. Fifty-six of the prisoners were charged or bailed to re-appear, whilst the remainder were given 'a stern warning to behave themselves in the future.'

The warning was ignored, and the Whitsuntide Bank Holiday in May saw much larger disturbances, this time in Brighton. Over 1,000 Mods and Rockers paraded up and down the seafront, mostly jostling holidaymakers but occasionally running into each other. On one such occasion some cornered Rockers had to jump across a wall and over the terrace to the road below, to escape the large group that was chasing them.

The street cred of the Rockers had taken a knock some weeks before, when a group of them had attacked a Boy Scouts' camp near Havering, slashing tents and destroying camping equipment.

Whilst those on the beach warmed themselves by the bonfires made of deckchairs, some of their number were staying warm in the police cells. There were seventy-five arrests for a variety of offences, and the courts were busy for several days clearing the backlog. Many of those arrested in this first outbreak in Brighton were actually local youths, although their numbers would decline considerably as a proportion in future

Mods not happy with the beach furniture feng shui during a Bank Holiday weekend in the sixties. (Reproduced with the kind permission of The Argus*)*

disturbances, once the movement had attracted a wider following.

One set of parents had been pleased when their son told them he was going to go camping at Littlehampton, as he didn't want to get involved in any bother in Brighton. They thought that he was at last showing some sense. Then the police knocked on their door to say that he had been arrested.

As shocking as the violence, for many of the older generation, was the discovery that many of those involved were taking drugs, particularly amphetamines. A survey by the Brighton Council of Youth revealed that 62 per cent of the Mods and 42 per cent of the Rockers were taking 'blues', a popular form of speed at the time. This may have explained why the Pope later that year described the faces

of Mods and Rockers as being 'filled with sorrow, vice, badness and delinquency'.

Further delinquency occurred the following year around the April and August Bank Holidays, and was met by a force of 100 policemen who had apparently been picked on the basis of their 'barn-door proportions'. The fresh misbehaviour inspired a range of possible solutions to the youth problem, at both a local and a national level.

One of the most popular solutions was an early usage of the now old 'national service' chestnut. Already the previous year a vicar had written in to *The Times*, calling for a return to conscription as a cure for these particular (and no doubt many other) societal ills. One father took this literally and had marched his son from the court straight to the army recruiting office, although the record doesn't state whether they took him in.

Some councillors on Brighton Council echoed the need for such an approach, involving a good dose of glasshouse discipline leavened with a liberal helping of hard labour. Presumably one young man from London was the exception that proved the military discipline rule. The recently demobbed ex-soldier got six months for breaking a motorist's nose and assaulting a policeman in East Street during the April troubles.

In the House of Lords a Labour peer proposed that the stocks should be brought back into use, to provide punishment and an entertainment for the holidaymakers. There were further outbreaks of trouble in the later part of the sixties, but fashions changed, and youth violence found a fresh arena in the nation's football grounds.

Whilst the Mod culture had survived to some extent in the north of England, particularly through dance around the Northern Soul circuit, in the south it had largely disappeared. This changed in the late 1970s, as a Mod revival, initially spurred by the post-punk Two-Tone movement, and then amplified by the release of the film *Quadrophenia*, took hold of much of the nation's youth.

If the fighting in the film looks real, it's not surprising, as many of the extras were going at it hammer and tongs on the beach, and most of them were from the new generation. In both 1980 and 1981 the seafront echoed again to the chants of large groups of youths, with large numbers of Mods this

time attempting to do battle with the skinheads, who had replaced Rockers as the enemy of choice. One of the more effective police tactics of this period was the enforced removal of bootlaces.

Again the papers searched for reasons to explain the violence. The Police Federation suggested that law and order had been undermined by the activities of civil liberties groups. Some might suggest that this mindset perhaps contributed to the widespread disturbances that occurred across the country the following year in 1981. The Police Federation would probably have suggested that such actions confirmed their position.

Mary Whitehouse, of course, had something to say, and she predictably blamed the levels of brutality on the television. Less predictably she may have actually had a point, although not in the way she intended. News coverage had already been suggested as generating copy-cat responses in the sixties, and there was much discussion of this thesis in the early eighties.

A more direct example of life imitating art came at a Mod dance held

Twenty-first-century Mods. (Maire McSorley)

LONG BACK AND SIDES

The Mods and Rockers may not have made many friends with their Bank Holiday behaviour, but they did have the support of the National Federation of Hairdressers Conference of 1964. The membership was urged to adapt its techniques to suit cults such as the Mods, Rockers and Beatles followers. Although there were some fears that longer hair would mean fewer visits to the barbers, the conference felt sure that business could be maintained if the members of such cults made sure they were well groomed.

The two groups who were really damaging the image of Britain, as seen from the barbershop floor, were apparently the beatniks and those dreaded social pariahs, the 'condescending television actor types'. Both groups were unpopular with the NHF because their unwashed and unkempt 'John the Baptist' and 'unemployed violinist' looks required little or no input from the scissor wielders.

Mr Wallace Snowcroft, president of the hairdressers, also suggested that prospective politicians should ensure that they had paid sufficient attention to their grooming when standing in an election: 'Voters are tired of those who believe that masses of woolly, straggly hair are a sign of intellectualism.'

The conference then unanimously approved a resolution to bring in variable charges, to educate the 'adolescent of today who thinks nothing of coming into our salons with 6 to 8 weeks of growth, expecting to pay only the minimum'.

in a Brighton club in 1981. A young man had been mimicking the balcony scene from *Quadrophenia*, when he fell onto the dance floor below. He spent the rest of the weekend in the Sussex County Hospital.

Within a few years, as before, the kids got older and the scene moved on, whilst the new generation had to suffer nearly a decade of the likes of Duran Duran, Jive Bunny and Rick Astley. Now that was a reason to take to the streets.

The beat goes on ... (DJB)